# New Vegetarian Gourmet Recipes

# New Vegetarian Gourmet Recipes

## Jean Conil

### Edited by: Barbara Croxford

## foulsham

London • New York • Toronto • Sydney

# foulsham

Yeovil Road, Slough, Berkshire, SL1 4JH

ISBN 0-572-01852-5

Typeset in Great Britain by Typesetting Solutions, Slough, Berks.
Printed in Great Britain by St. Edmundsbury Press, Bury St. Edmunds.

# ▼ Contents

# ▼
# *I*ntroduction

Vegetarianism is now beginning to be popular even with those people who thought it was not possible to survive on a meat-free diet. The unappealing image of life on nothing but nut cutlets is a thing of the past too as more cooks have brought their heads together to create a host of vegetarian recipes that would not disgrace the table of a Frenchman like me.

If you are vegetarian and believe in healthy eating, you can still enjoy all kinds of celebrations with food and drink. If you examine closely the enormous range of fruits and vegetables at our disposal, from our own country and from abroad, you can be thankful that you are alive and able to enjoy such a great natural harvest of food. Cereals are very important in a healthy diet, of course, and I have made a point of including cereal goodies in some of these entertaining dishes, at the same time cutting down on sugar and fat to fall into line with current beliefs about healthy eating.

Here are tempting and easy-to-follow gourmet recipes which will enable you to produce exciting and enjoyable celebration fare for your family and guests. This wealth of delectable vegetarian recipes is guaranteed to please even the most discriminating of gourmets. You can plan your own special occasion menus, choosing from sophisticated starters, delectable main courses and delightful desserts. The recipes use exotic fruits and vegetables available all year round and this splendid array of exotica will more than compensate for the absence of fish or meat. While you can be sure the recipes in this book are healthy vegetarian food, you will also find them perfect gourmet fare!

Bon appetit! *Jean Conil*

# 1

▼

# *S*tarters

## EXOTIC FRUIT COCKTAIL

Supermarkets now offer a wide selection of tropical fruits all year round so you can be certain of obtaining them whatever the season.

**Serves 4**

### ingredients

|  | Metric | Imperial | American |
|---|---|---|---|
| Mango | 1 | 1 | 1 |
| Papaya (pawpaw) | 1 | 1 | 1 |
| Kiwi fruit (Chinese gooseberries) | 2 | 2 | 2 |
| Bananas | 2 small | 2 small | 2 small |
| Juice of 1 lime | | | |

**Decoration**
Sprig of mint
Cranberries,
   fresh or frozen

### method

1. Using a sharp knife, peel the mango and papaya (pawpaw). Remove the stone (pit) and seeds and cut in thin slices.

2. Peel and slice the kiwi fruit and bananas.

3. Combine the fruits and arrange in individual serving bowls or glasses. Decorate with mint leaves and cranberries.

4. Chill until required and, just before serving, squeeze lime juice over each portion.

# BEIGNETS DE BRIE A LA NOIX DE COCO

*Deep-fried Brie with Coconut*

These delicious Brie or Camembert fritters should be cooked just before eating. They make a very festive special occasion starter.

**Serves 6**

## ingredients

|  | Metric | Imperial | American |
|---|---|---|---|
| Brie or Camembert cheese | 450 g | 1 lb | 1 lb |
| Plain (all-purpose) flour | 2 tbsp | 2 tbsp | 2 tbsp |
| Celery seeds or salt | 1 tsp | 1 tsp | 1 tsp |
| Eggs, beaten | 2 | 2 | 2 |
| Desiccated (shredded) coconut | 50 g | 2 oz | ⅔ cup |
| Oil for deep frying |  |  |  |

**Garnish**
Celery stalks
Mouli (Japanese white radish) slices

## method

1.   Cut the cheese into 12 small triangles. Season the flour with celery seeds or salt. Coat the cheese triangles with seasoned flour, then dip in beaten egg and roll in desiccated (shredded) coconut.

2.   Heat the oil and deep-fry the cheese triangles for 1 minute until golden brown. Drain well on absorbent kitchen paper.

3.   Arrange on serving plates with slices of mouli (Japanese white radish) and stalks of celery. Serve immediately.

# MUSHROOM AND HERB PATE

This mouthwatering pâté is best served on lettuce leaves with garlic bread or wholewheat toast. It is also delicious served as a dip.

*Serves 6*

## ingredients

|  | Metric | Imperial | American |
|---|---|---|---|
| *Oil* | *2 tbsp* | *2 tbsp* | *2 tbsp* |
| *Onion, chopped* | *1 small* | *1 small* | *1 small* |
| *Garlic cloves, chopped* | *2* | *2* | *2* |
| *Mushrooms, trimmed and sliced* | *225 g* | *8 oz* | *2 cups* |
| *Tomato purée (paste)* | *1 tsp* | *1 tsp* | *1 tsp* |
| *Mixed chopped fresh herbs, e.g. coriander basil, mint, tarragon, parsley, marjoram* | *1 tbsp* | *1 tbsp* | *1 tbsp* |
| *Eggs, beaten* | *2* | *2* | *2* |
| *Salt and freshly milled black pepper* | | | |
| *Breadcrumbs* | *2 tbsp* | *2 tbsp* | *2 tbsp* |
| *Lettuce leaves* | *6* | *6* | *6* |
| *Coriander leaves to garnish* | | | |

## method

1.  Heat the oil in a frying-pan (skillet) and stir-fry the onion and garlic for 2 minutes until soft but not brown.

2.  Add the mushrooms and cook for 4 minutes, then blend in the tomato purée (paste) and herbs.

3.  Season the beaten eggs with salt and pepper to taste, pour into the pan and cook gently, stirring, until lightly scrambled. Stir in the breadcrumbs.

4.  Transfer the mixture to a blender or food processor and blend to a smooth purée. (If a coarser texture is preferred, blend for only a few seconds, or put the mixture through a mincer/meat grinder instead.)

5.  Arrange the lettuce leaves on three serving plates and place spoonfuls of the pâté in the centre of each. Garnish with coriander leaves and serve with garlic bread or wholewheat toast.

# SKORDALIA A LA GRECQUE

Crudités and dips are a must for celebration parties. Make sure you have a large assortment of vegetables and fruit to serve with this dip. It is made with mayonnaise.

**Serves 4**

## ingredients

|  | Metric | Imperial | American |
|---|---|---|---|
| Mayonnaise | 225 ml | 8 fl oz | 1 cup |
| Garlic cloves, chopped | 2 | 2 | 2 |
| Walnuts, chopped | 2 | 2 | 2 |
| Breadcrumbs | 25 g | 1 oz | ½ cup |
| Juice of ½ lemon | | | |
| Plain yogurt | 2 tbsp | 2 tbsp | 2 tbsp |
| Sesame (benne) seeds, toasted | 1 tbsp | 1 tbsp | 1 tbsp |
| Chopped fresh basil | 2 tsp | 2 tsp | 2 tsp |

**Crudités**

| | | | |
|---|---|---|---|
| Small cauliflower florets (flowerets) | | | |
| Button mushrooms | | | |
| Celery stalks, cut in batons | 2 | 2 | 2 |
| Carrots, cut in batons | 2 | 2 | 2 |
| Fennel bulbs, cut in batons | 2 | 2 | 2 |
| Mouli (Japanese white radish), thickly sliced | 1 | 1 | 1 |
| Mangetouts (snow peas) or French (green) beans | | | |
| Slices of apple and pear | | | |

## method

1. Combine the mayonnaise with the garlic, walnuts, breadcrumbs, lemon juice, yogurt, sesame (benne) seeds and

basil. Place in a blender or food processor and purée until smooth. Pour into one large or two small bowls to serve.

2.   Arrange the crudités decoratively on a serving plate and serve with the dip.

# PINEAPPLE HONOLULU

Pineapple with cottage cheese surrounded by tangy mushrooms.

**Serves 4**

### ingredients

|  | Metric | Imperial | American |
|---|---|---|---|
| Lettuce leaves | 4 | 4 | 4 |
| Radicchio leaves | 4 | 4 | 4 |
| Pineapple slices, cored | 4 | 4 | 4 |
| Mushrooms, sliced | 150 g | 5 oz | 1¼ cups |
| Cottage cheese | 175 g | 6 oz | ¾ cup |
| **Marinade** | | | |
| Worcestershire sauce | 2 tbsp | 2 tbsp | 2 tbsp |
| Onion, chopped | 1 small | 1 small | 1 small |
| Fresh root ginger, peeled and grated | 1 tsp | 1 tsp | 1 tsp |
| Pineapple slice | 1 | 1 | 1 |
| Sunflower oil | 2 tbsp | 2 tbsp | 2 tbsp |

### method

1.   Arrange the lettuce and radicchio leaves on four plates and top with a slice of pineapple.

2.   Place all the marinade ingredients in a blender or food processor and blend together. Pour over the mushrooms and toss for a few minutes.

3.   Place a spoonful of cottage cheese on top of each pineapple slice and spoon mushrooms all around.

# MUSHROOMS IN CHAMPAGNE VELOUTE WITH QUAIL EGGS

The secret of the lovely sauce for this sophisticated first course lies in its rapid reduction and in the careful blending of herbs.

## Serves 4

### ingredients

| | Metric | Imperial | American |
|---|---|---|---|
| Quail eggs | 4 | 4 | 4 |
| **Sauce** | | | |
| Oil | 1½ tbsp | 1½ tbsp | 1½ tbsp |
| Shallots, chopped | 2 small | 2 small | 2 small |
| Button mushrooms, wiped and trimmed | 225 g | 8 oz | 2 cups |
| Sparkling wine or champagne | 150 ml | ¼ pint | ⅔ cup |
| Cornflour (cornstarch) | ½ tsp | ½ tsp | ½ tsp |
| Sour cream | 75 ml | 2½ fl oz | 5 tbsp |
| Mixed chopped fresh chervil, coriander and mint | 1 tbsp | 1 tbsp | 1 tbsp |
| Salt and freshly milled black pepper | | | |
| Cucumber, cut in 6 mm/¼ inch cubes | 150 g | 5 oz | 1¼ cups |
| Head of chicory (endive) leaves separated | 1 | 1 | 1 |
| Ground turmeric and paprika to flavour | | | |

### method

1. Cook the quail eggs in boiling water for 6 minutes. Shell, place in a bowl and cover with warm water.

2. To make the sauce, heat the oil in a small saucepan, add the shallots and stir-fry for 1 minute, without browning.

3.  Add the mushrooms and toss in oil for 2 minutes, then remove with a slotted spoon and keep warm.

4.  Add the sparkling wine or champagne and boil rapidly for 10 minutes to reduce by half.

5.  Stir the cornflour (cornstarch) into the sour cream and add to the pan with the herbs. Boil for 4 minutes, stirring, until thickened.

6.  Season to taste with salt and pepper and add the mushrooms and cucumber. Simmer for 2 minutes only.

7.  Spoon into the centre of four serving plates and arrange the chicory (endive) leaves all around in a petal pattern.

8.  Cut the quail eggs in half and arrange two in the centre of each plate. Sprinkle with a mixture of turmeric and paprika.

**Variation**
For contrast, alternate the chicory leaves with large coriander leaves.

# COURGETTE FRITTERS WITH YOGURT SAUCE

These lightly sautéed courgette batons are coated in a garlic, almond and breadcrumb mixture.

*Serves 4*

## ingredients

|  | Metric | Imperial | American |
|---|---|---|---|
| *Courgettes (zucchini)* | *4 small* | *4 small* | *4 small* |
| *Plain (all-purpose) flour* | *4 tbsp* | *4 tbsp* | *4 tbsp* |
| *Salt and freshly milled black pepper* | | | |
| *Wholewheat breadcrumbs* | *50 g* | *2 oz* | *½ cup* |
| *Nibbed almonds* | *50 g* | *2 oz* | *½ cup* |
| *Garlic clove, crushed* | *1* | *1* | *1* |
| *Eggs, beaten* | *2* | *2* | *2* |
| *Oil for shallow frying* | | | |

**Yogurt sauce**

|  | Metric | Imperial | American |
|---|---|---|---|
| *Cucumber, roughly chopped* | *100 g* | *4 oz* | *1 cup* |
| *Garlic clove, peeled* | *1* | *1* | *1* |
| *Plain yogurt* | *100 ml* | *4 fl oz* | *½ cup* |
| *Salt and freshly milled black pepper* | | | |

## method

1.  First make the sauce. Place all the ingredients in a blender or food processor and blend well. Transfer to a small serving bowl.

2.  Trim the courgettes (zucchini) and cut in batons about 5 cm/ 2 inches long and 6 mm/¼ inch wide.

3.   Season the flour with salt and pepper and mix the breadcrumbs and nuts on a plate. Beat the crushed garlic into the eggs.

4.   Coat the courgette batons with seasoned flour, then dip in beaten egg and roll in breadcrumbs and nuts.

5.   Heat oil in a frying-pan (skillet) and quickly sauté the coated courgette batons for 1 minute. Remove from the pan and drain well on absorbent kitchen paper. Serve immediately with yogurt sauce.

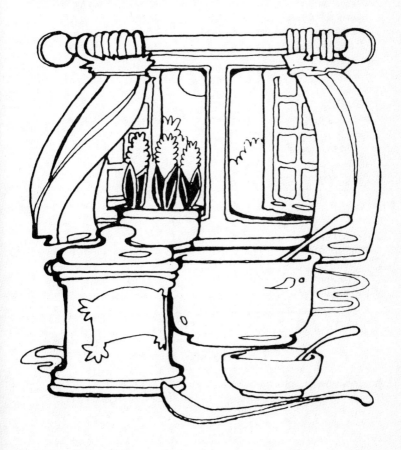

# PANIR DUMPLINGS

Making ideal buffet party fare, these dumplings are spicy with a creamy centre.

## Serves 6

### ingredients

|  | Metric | Imperial | American |
|---|---|---|---|
| Cream cheese, softened | 450 g | 1 lb | 2 cups |
| Eggs, beaten | 2 | 2 | 2 |
| Breadcrumbs | 50 g | 2 oz | 1 cup |
| Onion, chopped | 1 small | 1 small | 1 small |
| Garlic clove, chopped | 1 small | 1 small | 1 small |
| Chopped fresh basil or mint | 1 tbsp | 1 tbsp | 1 tbsp |
| Oil for deep frying | | | |

**Coating**

|  | | | |
|---|---|---|---|
| Wholewheat flour | 3 tbsp | 3 tbsp | 3 tbsp |
| Salt and freshly milled black pepper | | | |
| Egg, beaten | 1 | 1 | 1 |
| Plain yogurt | 3 tbsp | 3 tbsp | 3 tbsp |
| Curry powder | 1 tsp | 1 tsp | 1 tsp |
| Nibbed almonds | 50 g | 2 oz | ½ cup |

**To serve**

|  | | | |
|---|---|---|---|
| Pineapple cubes, fresh or drained canned | 150 g | 5 oz | 1 cup |
| Cocktail sticks (wooden picks) | | | |

### method

1.  In a bowl, combine the cream cheese, beaten eggs, breadcrumbs, onion, garlic and herbs and blend to a paste. Divide the mixture and roll into small balls.

2.    For the coating, season the flour with salt and pepper and beat together the egg, yogurt and curry powder. Roll the balls in seasoned flour, then dip in egg and yogurt mixture and finally roll in nibbed almonds.

3.    Heat the oil and deep-fry the cheese balls for 1 minute until golden. Drain well on absorbent kitchen paper.

4.    Serve the cheese balls on cocktail sticks (wooden picks) with a cube of pineapple added to each one.

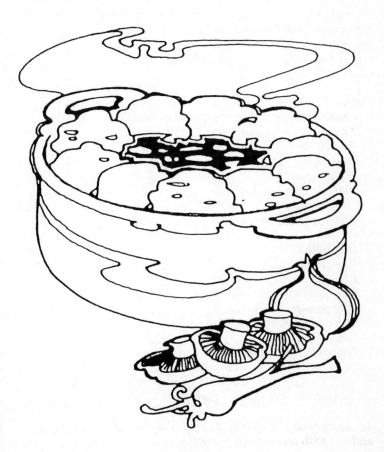

# 2

# *M*ain Courses

## ROULADE FLORENTINE

This impressive roulade is filled with a combination of spinach, mushrooms and cashew nuts lightly coated in yogurt.

### Serves 6 — ingredients

|  | Metric | Imperial | American |
|---|---|---|---|
| Oil | 2 tbsp | 2 tbsp | 2 tbsp |
| Onion, chopped | 1 medium | 1 medium | 1 medium |
| Mushrooms, chopped | 4 | 4 | 4 |
| Leaf spinach, chopped | 100 g | 4 oz | ½ cup |
| Cashew nuts, chopped | 50 g | 2 oz | ½ cup |
| Plain yogurt | 75 ml | 2½ fl oz | 5 tbsp |
| Salt and freshly milled black pepper | | | |
| Watercress to garnish | | | |

**Roulade**

|  | | | |
|---|---|---|---|
| Eggs, separated | 5 | 5 | 5 |
| Cheddar cheese, grated | 50 g | 2 oz | ½ cup |
| Chopped fresh coriander or parsley | 2 tbsp | 2 tbsp | 2 tbsp |
| Salt and freshly milled black pepper | | | |
| Grated Parmesan | | | |

### method

1.  Lightly oil a 23 x 33 cm/9 x 13 inch Swiss (jelly) roll tin (pan) and line with greaseproof (waxed) paper.

2.   Heat oil in a frying-pan (skillet) and sauté the onion for 2 minutes with browning. Add mushrooms, spinach and cashew nuts and cook for 5 minutes. Stir in the yogurt and boil for 2 minutes more. Season to taste with salt and pepper and leave to cool.

3.   Preheat the oven to 200°C/400°F/Gas Mark 6.

4.   Place the egg yolks, grated cheese, herbs and a pinch of pepper in a bowl and beat together.

5.   Place the egg whites in a large bowl with a pinch of salt and whisk until stiff enough to cling to the whisk. Fold carefully into the egg yolk mixture.

6.   Pour the roulade mixture into the prepared tin and spread evenly. Smooth the surface with a palette knife. Bake in the oven for 10 minutes then remove from the oven and leave to cool.

7.   Place a sheet of greaseproof paper on a working surface and sprinkle with grated Parmesan. Turn the roulade out onto the sheet of paper and peel off the lining paper.

8.   Spread the spinach mixture evenly over the roulade and roll up like a Swiss roll, using the sheet of greaseproof paper underneath to help.

9.   Lift the whole roulade carefully into a serving dish or cut in slices and serve on individual plates. Garnish with watercress.

# LASAGNE VERDI

This is a mouthwatering vegetarian version of a very famous pasta dish that you can make in winter as well as in summer as it uses frozen spinach and canned tomatoes. Oblong sheets of green lasagne can be bought in 450 g/1 lb packets (packages). Do not boil them in a small saucepan as they will stick. Instead, use a shallow roasting tin (pan) which will hold 1.2 litres/2 pints/5 cups of boiling water and cook the lasagne sheets separately.

## Serves 4 — ingredients

|  | Metric | Imperial | American |
|---|---|---|---|
| Water | 1.2 litres | 2 pints | 5 cups |
| Oil | 1 tbsp | 1 tbsp | 1 tbsp |
| Pinch of salt |  |  |  |
| Lasagne verdi | 225 g | 8 oz | ½ lb |
| **Filling** |  |  |  |
| Oil | 3 tbsp | 3 tbsp | 3 tbsp |
| Red onion, sliced | 1 | 1 | 1 |
| Frozen spinach, thawed | 225 g | 8 oz | ½ lb |
| Juice of ½ lemon |  |  |  |
| Grated nutmeg |  |  |  |
| Canned tomatoes, drained and sliced | 225 g | 8 oz | ½ lb |
| Walnuts | 150 g | 5 oz | 1 cup |
| Salt and freshly milled black pepper |  |  |  |
| **Topping** |  |  |  |
| Plain yogurt | 150 ml | 5 fl oz | ⅔ cup |
| Milk or water | 3 tbsp | 3 tbsp | 3 tbsp |
| Gruyère or Cheddar cheese, grated | 150 g | 5 oz | 1¼ cups |

## method

1.   Boil the water in a large shallow roasting tin (pan) and add oil and salt.

2.   Cook eight sheets of lasagne, slipping them into the boiling water one at a time and boiling for 6 minutes each. Remove with a fish slice (slotted spatula) and place in a bowl of cold water to cool.

3.   When cold, spread out the lasagne sheets on a clean cloth and leave to dry. Grease a 1.2 litre/2 pint/5 cup ovenproof pie dish with a little oil or margarine.

4.   For the filling, heat the oil in a frying-pan (skillet) and stir-fry the onion for 4 minutes until soft but not brown. Remove from the heat. Preheat the oven to 200°C/400°F/ Gas Mark 6.

5.   Season the spinach with lemon juice and nutmeg and spread half in the bottom of the pie dish. Cover with a layer of cooked lasagne followed by a layer of half the tomatoes.

6.   Arrange a layer of half the onion on top of the tomatoes in the pie dish, add half the walnuts and season to taste with salt and pepper. Cover with another layer of lasagne then repeat layers of spinach, lasagne, tomato, onion and walnuts, and finish with a layer of lasagne.

7.   For the topping, beat the yogurt with the milk or water and pour over the lasagne. Sprinkle with grated cheese. Bake in the oven for 20-25 minutes until golden and bubbling.

# TIMBALE DE RIZ AUX GRAINES DE CITROUILLE

For a more spectacular presentation of this unusual dish, pack the hot mixture into individual star, round or oblong moulds (molds) and invert like sandcastles onto serving plates.

**Serves 4**

## ingredients

| | Metric | Imperial | American |
|---|---|---|---|
| Mung beans | 225 g | 8 oz | ½ lb |
| Polyunsaturated oil | 3 tbsp | 3 tbsp | 3 tbsp |
| Red onion, chopped | 1 | 1 | 1 |
| Garlic cloves, crushed | 2 | 2 | 2 |
| Long-grain rice | 225 g | 8 oz | ½ lb |
| Ground turmeric | 1 tsp | 1 tsp | 1 tsp |
| Yeast extract | 1 tsp | 1 tsp | 1 tsp |
| Hot water | 750 ml | 1¼ pints | 3 cups |
| Salt and freshly milled black pepper | | | |
| Pumpkin seeds | 1 tbsp | 1 tbsp | 1 tbsp |
| Pumpkin pulp, cut into 6 mm/¼ inch cubes | 150 g | 5 oz | 1 cup |
| Mixed chopped fresh herbs, e.g. basil, mint, lemon balm, parsley, marjoram | 3 tbsp | 3 tbsp | 3 tbsp |

### Garnish

| | | | |
|---|---|---|---|
| Plums, halved and stoned (pitted) | 8 | 8 | 8 |
| Sprigs of fresh coriander | | | |

## method

1. Place the beans in a bowl, cover with cold water and leave to soak for 2 hours.

2.   Drain the beans, rinse in fresh cold water and drain again.

3.   Heat the oil in a large frying-pan (skillet) and stir-fry the onion and garlic for 1 minute until soft but not brown. Stir in the beans, rice and turmeric and cook, stirring, for 2 minutes to allow the flavours to blend.

4.   Dissolve the yeast extract in the hot water and pour into the pan. Cook gently for 35-40 minutes until rice and beans are tender and the water has been absorbed. Season to taste with salt and pepper.

5.   While the rice and beans are cooking, heat a little oil in a frying-pan and fry the pumpkin seeds until browned. Drain on absorbent kitchen paper.

6.   Cook the pumpkin pulp in boiling water for 6 minutes until tender and drain well.

7.   Spoon the cooked rice and bean mixture onto four heated serving plates and surround with plum halves. Sprinkle with fried pumpkin seeds.

8.   Pile the cooked pumpkin on top and sprinkle with chopped fresh herbs. Serve while still hot, garnished with a sprig of coriander.

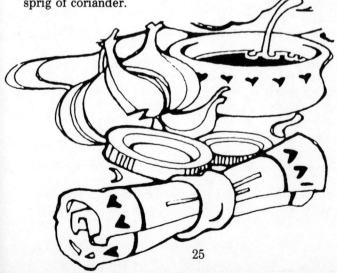

# RISOTTO JAPANESE

It is interesting that a French chef like me should take to oriental food with such enthusiasm. It is clean, healthy and artistic, so it is no wonder really that it should appeal. To make up the protein, I have added tofu (soya bean curd) to this rice dish with a garnish of grapes and satsumas.

## Serves 4

### ingredients

| | Metric | Imperial | American |
|---|---|---|---|
| Polyunsaturated margarine | 50 g | 2 oz | ¼ cup |
| Red onion, chopped | 1 | 1 | 1 |
| Patna rice | 225 g | 8 oz | ½ lb |
| Preserved ginger, chopped | 1 tbsp | 1 tbsp | 1 tbsp |
| Ground turmeric | ¼ tsp | ¼ tsp | ¼ tsp |
| Salt and freshly milled black pepper or a dash of soy sauce | | | |
| Hot water | 600 ml | 1 pint | 2½ cups |
| Red chilli (chili pepper), seeded and sliced | 1 | 1 | 1 |
| Tofu, cut in cubes | 225 g | 8 oz | ½ lb |
| **Garnish** | | | |
| Seedless grapes | 50 g | 2 oz | ½ cup |
| Satsumas or similar fruits, peeled and segmented | 1-2 | 1-2 | 1-2 |

### method

1.  Heat the margarine in a saucepan and stir-fry the onion for 2 minutes until soft. Add the rice and ginger and stir to coat well with fat.

2.   Add the turmeric, salt and pepper or soy sauce to taste, and the hot water. Bring to the boil and cook gently for 10 minutes.

3.   Add the chilli and tofu and continue cooking for a further 10 minutes.

4.   Serve on individual plates garnished with satsumas and grapes.

# CHOUX FARCIS A LA CONIL

*Stuffed Cabbage à la Conil*

My grandmother made these delicious stuffed cabbage parcels by the hundred from the produce of her own garden. Filled with dried apricots, cottage cheese and nuts, they make a satisfying, entertaining main dish.

| Serves 4 **ingredients** | | | |
|---|---|---|---|
| | Metric | Imperial | American |
| Cabbage leaves | 4 large | 4 large | 4 large |
| **Stuffing** | | | |
| Dried apricots or peaches | 150 g | 5 oz | 1 cup |
| Cottage cheese | 150 g | 5 oz | ½ cup |
| Egg, beaten | 1 | 1 | 1 |
| Wholewheat breadcrumbs | 50 g | 2 oz | 1 cup |
| Mixed walnuts and hazelnuts, chopped | 150 g | 5 oz | 1 cup |
| Pinch of ground mixed spice | | | |
| Salt and freshly milled black pepper | | | |
| **Sauce (Coulis de tomates)** | | | |
| Oil | 2 tbsp | 2 tbsp | 2 tbsp |
| Onion, chopped | 1 small | 1 small | 1 small |
| Tomatoes, peeled and chopped | 2 large | 2 large | 2 large |
| Pinch of oregano | | | |
| Salt and freshly milled black pepper | | | |
| Cornflour (cornstarch) | 1 tsp | 1 tsp | 1 tsp |
| Water | 3 tbsp | 3 tbsp | 3 tbsp |

## method

1.   Place the dried apricots or peaches in a bowl, cover with water and leave to soak for 2 hours. Drain well and put through a mincer (meat grinder) or chop finely in a food processor.

2.   Trim the centre cores from the cabbage leaves and blanch the leaves in boiling water for 30 seconds. Spread the leaves out on a board ready to be filled.

3.   To make the stuffing, place the cottage cheese in a bowl and blend it with the beaten egg and breadcrumbs. Add the apricots or peaches, nuts and spice, season with salt and pepper and mix well.

4.   Divide the stuffing mixture into four portions and place one on each cabbage leaf. Wrap the leaves round the stuffing to make neat parcels. Arrange in an ovenproof dish. Preheat the oven to 200°C/400°F/Gas Mark 6.

5.   For the sauce, heat the frying-pan (skillet) and stir-fry the onion for 4 minutes until soft but not brown. Add the tomatoes and oregano and season to taste with salt and pepper. Simmer for 10 minutes.

6.   Blend the cornflour (cornstarch) and water and add to the sauce mixture. Cook for a further 3 minutes, stirring, until thickened.

7.   Check the seasoning then pour the sauce around the cabbage parcels. Bake in the oven for 15 minutes and serve very hot with creamed potatoes.

# PANE AGRO DOLCE

This delicious savoury pie made with yeast dough is filled with a mixture of courgettes (zucchini) and tomatoes with oregano and mint.

## Serves 4 — ingredients

| | Metric | Imperial | American |
|---|---|---|---|
| Strong plain (all-purpose) flour | 225 g | 8 oz | 2 cups |
| Salt | ½ tsp | ½ tsp | ½ tsp |
| Milk | 150 ml | ¼ pint | ⅔ cup |
| Sachet dried yeast (active dry yeast) | 1 | 1 | 1 |
| Egg, beaten | 1 | 1 | 1 |
| Oil | 1 tbsp | 1 tbsp | 1 tbsp |
| Milk or beaten yolk to glaze | | | |
| Sesame (benne) seeds | 1 tbsp | 1 tbsp | 1 tbsp |
| Lettuce to garnish | | | |

### Filling

| | Metric | Imperial | American |
|---|---|---|---|
| Oil | 3 tbsp | 3 tbsp | 3 tbsp |
| Onion, chopped | 1 large | 1 large | 1 large |
| Garlic cloves, chopped | 2 | 2 | 2 |
| Tomatoes, peeled, seeded and chopped | 2 | 2 | 2 |
| Courgette (zucchini), sliced | 1 | 1 | 1 |
| Salt and freshly milled black pepper | | | |
| Fresh mint leaves, chopped or chopped tarragon | | | |
| Oregano | 1 tsp | 1 tsp | 1 tsp |
| Sesame (benne) seeds | 1 tbsp | 1 tbsp | 1 tbsp |

## method

1.   First prepare the dough. Sift the flour and salt together into a bowl and make a well in the centre.

2.   Heat the milk to blood heat (but no hotter), sprinkle in the yeast and stir. Pour into the well in the flour, cover with a clean cloth and leave to stand for 15 minutes until the yeast starts foaming.

3.   Add beaten egg and oil to the yeast mixture and beat to a dough. Knead well, shape into a ball, cover again and leave to rise for 45 minutes.

4.   Meanwhile, prepare the filling. Heat the oil in a frying-pan (skillet) and stir-fry the onion for 2 minutes until slightly golden.

5.   Add the garlic and tomatoes and simmer for 12 minutes. Add courgette (zucchini) and cook for a further 3 minutes only. Season to taste with salt and pepper and herbs and leave to cool.

6.   Grease a round 18 cm/7 inch cake tin (pan) with a little oil.

7.   Turn the dough onto a lightly floured surface and knock back (punch down). Divide into two and roll one piece into an 18 cm/7 inch round. Roll the other into a round large enough to line the bottom and sides of the cake tin.

8.   Use the larger piece of dough to line the bottom and sides of the prepared tin and prick the bottom all over with a fork. Fill with the courgette and tomato mixture and cover with the second round of dough.

9.   Brush with milk or beaten egg yolk and sprinkle with sesame (benne) seeds. Leave to rest for 25 minutes, then bake in the oven at 200°C/400°F/Gas Mark 6 for 20-25 minutes until golden.

10.   To serve, cut into triangles and garnish with lettuce.

# ALGERIAN COUSCOUS

During my conscripted service in the French Navy I spent many months visiting the North African countries and I must confess I have become very fond of couscous. It is similar to semolina and is served with vegetables. I find it far more tasty and nutritious than rice. I have adapted this dish in which couscous is cooked and served with a leek and fennel casserole.

## Serves 4

### ingredients

|  | Metric | Imperial | American |
|---|---|---|---|
| *Leeks, trimmed and cut in chunks* | 2 | 2 | 2 |
| *Fennel bulb, trimmed and sliced* | 1 small | 1 small | 1 small |
| *Tomatoes, peeled, seeded and chopped* | 2 large | 2 large | 2 large |
| *Can of chick-peas, drained* | 400 g | 14 oz | 2 cups |
| *Carrots, peeled and thinly sliced* | 2 | 2 | 2 |
| *Celery stalk, sliced* | 1 | 1 | 1 |
| *Green chilli (chili pepper), seeded and sliced* | 1 | 1 | 1 |
| *Good pinch of cumin* |  |  |  |
| *Garlic cloves, crushed* | 2 | 2 | 2 |
| *Sprig of fresh mint* |  |  |  |
| *Tomato purée (paste)* | 2 tbsp | 2 tbsp | 2 tbsp |
| *Salt* |  |  |  |
| *Vegetable stock (bouillon) cubes* | 2 | 2 | 2 |
| *Hot water* | 1 litre | 1¾ pints | 4¼ cups |
| **Couscous** |  |  |  |
| *Couscous* | 225 g | 8 oz | ½ lb |
| *Polyunsaturated margarine* | 50 g | 2 oz | ¼ cup |

| | | | |
|---|---|---|---|
| *Frozen peas and sweetcorn (whole kernel corn) mix, cooked* | *50 g* | *2 oz* | *¾ cup* |
| *Seedless raisins* | *50 g* | *2 oz* | *⅓ cup* |
| *Split blanched almonds, lightly toasted* | *50 g* | *2 oz* | *½ cup* |
| *Salt and freshly milled black pepper* | | | |

**To serve (optional)**
*Watermelon*
*Fresh dates*

## method

1.   Place the leeks, fennel, tomatoes, chick-peas, carrots, celery, chilli, cumin, garlic, mint and tomato purée (paste) in a large saucepan. Season with salt, crumble in the vegetable stock (bouillon) cubes and add the hot water. Bring to the boil and simmer for 25 minutes until the vegetables are tender.

2.   Drain off 300 ml/½ pint/1¼ cups vegetable stock and pour into a jug (pitcher).

3.   To cook couscous, heat the margarine in a sauté pan, add the couscous and heat gently, stirring, for 3 minutes. Gradually add the 300 ml/½ pint/1¼ cups stock and cook for 6 minutes. Transfer to a dish and leave to stand for 10 minutes.

4.   Stir the cooked peas and sweetcorn, the raisins and the almonds into the couscous, mix well and season to taste with salt and pepper.

5.   Divide the vegetables between four soup plates and add a little vegetable cooking stock to each. Serve the couscous separately in individual dishes.

6.   To be truly authentic, serve wedges of watermelon and fresh dates with this couscous dish. The Arabs eat the watermelon seeds as well as they are very nutritious.

# GATEAU AU FROMAGE BRETONNE

This spectacular dish is made by piling up pancakes (crêpes) sandwiched together with cream cheese, tomatoes and lettuce leaves. Perfect for a summer celebration.

## Serves 4 — ingredients

|  | Metric | Imperial | American |
|---|---|---|---|
| Plain (all-purpose) flour | 100g | 4 oz | 1 cup |
| Ground almonds | 25 g | 1 oz | ¼ cup |
| Eggs, beaten | 2 | 2 | 2 |
| Milk and water | 300 ml | ½ pint | 1¼ cups |
| Chopped fresh parsley | 1 tbsp | 1 tbsp | 1 tbsp |
| Salt |  |  |  |
| Oil |  |  |  |
| **Filling** |  |  |  |
| Cream cheese, softened | 75 g | 3 oz | ½ cup |
| Plain yogurt | 1½ tbsp | 1½ tbsp | 1½ tbsp |
| Caraway seeds | 1 tsp | 1 tsp | 1 tsp |
| Tomatoes, sliced | 2 large | 2 large | 2 large |
| Lettuce leaves | 4 | 4 | 4 |
| Thin slices of Gruyère cheese | 3 | 3 | 3 |
| **Dressing** |  |  |  |
| Plain yogurt | 150 ml | 5 fl oz | ⅔ cup |
| Cucumber, chopped | 150 g | 5 oz | 1¼ cups |
| Salt and freshly milled black pepper |  |  |  |

## method

1. Place the flour and ground almonds in a bowl, beat in the eggs and gradually beat in the milk. Season with chopped parsley and a pinch of salt.

2. Heat 1 tablespoon oil in a small omelette pan or frying-pan (skillet), measuring about 16 cm/6½ inches across. Pour in 75 ml/2½ fl oz/5 tbsp of the batter mixture. Cook for about 2 minutes until the underside is golden, then turn and cook the other side. Repeat until all the batter has been used, making about eight pancakes (crêpes). Leave to cool.

3. For the filling, beat together the cream cheese, yogurt and caraway seeds.

4. Place a pancake on a 20 cm/8 inch serving plate and spread with a layer of caraway-flavoured cream cheese. Cover with another pancake and arrange slices of tomato, lettuce leaves and Gruyère cheese on top. Add a third pancake and spread with cream cheese mixture. Repeat the layers until all the ingredients have been used. Press down slightly, using another plate.

5. To make the dressing, simply combine the yogurt and cucumber in a blender or food processor and season to taste with salt and pepper. Serve with the gâteau cut in wedges like a cake.

# HUNGARIAN VEGETABLE GOULASH

You don't need meat to make a goulash as tasty as the traditional Hungarian original. Ideal for winter entertaining, this hearty vegetable casserole combines vegetables with beans or peas for extra protein.

**Serves 4** — **ingredients**

| | Metric | Imperial | American |
|---|---|---|---|
| Sunflower oil | 4 tbsp | 4 tbsp | 4 tbsp |
| Red onions, coarsely chopped | 2 | 2 | 2 |
| Garlic cloves, chopped | 2 | 2 | 2 |
| Paprika | 1 tbsp | 1 tbsp | 1 tbsp |
| Celery stalks, sliced | 2 | 2 | 2 |
| Carrots, peeled and sliced | 2 | 2 | 2 |
| Parsnips, peeled and sliced | 2 | 2 | 2 |
| Turnips or swedes (rutabaga), peeled and cut in 2.5 cm/ 1 inch cubes | 2 | 2 | 2 |
| Red pepper, seeded and cut in squares | 1 | 1 | 1 |
| Potatoes, peeled and cut into 2.5 cm/1 inch cubes | 225 g | 8 oz | ½ lb |
| Water | 600 ml | 1 pint | 2½ cups |
| Tomato purée (paste) | 2 tbsp | 2 tbsp | 2 tbsp |
| Vegetable stock (bouillon) cubes | 2 | 2 | 2 |
| Sprig of thyme or sage | | | |
| Baked beans or cooked peas | 75 g | 3 oz | ½ cup |
| Cornflour (cornstarch) | 2 tsp | 2 tsp | 2 tsp |

| | | | |
|---|---|---|---|
| *Plain yogurt* | *150 ml* | *5 fl oz* | *⅔ cup* |
| *Salt and freshly milled black pepper* | | | |
| *Chopped fresh parsley to garnish* | | | |
| **Dumplings** | | | |
| *Self-raising flour* | *225 g* | *8 oz* | *2 cups* |
| *Vegetable margarine* | *100 g* | *4 oz* | *½ cup* |
| *Caraway seeds* | *1 tsp* | *1 tsp* | *1 tsp* |
| *Salt* | *¼ tsp* | *¼ tsp* | *¼ tsp* |
| *Egg* | *1* | *1* | *1* |
| *Warm water* | *2 tbsp* | *2 tbsp* | *2 tbsp* |

## method

1. Heat the oil in a large heavy-based saucepan and stir-fry the onion and garlic for 5 minutes until soft but not brown.

2. Sprinkle in paprika and add all other vegetables (except the baked beans or cooked peas). Cover with water and bring to the boil.

3. Stir in the tomato purée (paste) and crumble in the vegetable stock (bouillon) cubes. Add thyme or sage, cover and boil gently for 15 minutes.

4. Stir in the beans or peas. In a cup, blend the cornflour (cornstarch) with the yogurt (diluted with 4 tablespoons water if too firm) and stir into the vegetable mixture. Simmer for 5 minutes more until thickened. Check seasoning.

5. The dumplings are best cooked separately in a shallow metal tray or pan. Place flour and margarine in a bowl and rub (cut) in the margarine.

6. Add caraway seeds and salt and bind with egg and water. Roll the dough into 12 balls the size of walnuts.

7. Cook in boiling salted water in a shallow tray or pan for 6-8 minutes. Remove with a slotted spoon.

8. Transfer the vegetable casserole to a large heated serving dish or serve straight into heated soup plates. Top with caraway dumplings and sprinkle with chopped parsley.

# MERIDIONAL MEDLEY

Here is a colourful platter of stuffed vegetables to satisfy both appetite and taste with a variety of fillings. Your guests can choose their favourites.

**Serves 4** — **ingredients**

|  | Metric | Imperial | American |
|---|---|---|---|
| Tomatoes | 2 large | 2 large | 2 large |
| Aubergine (eggplant) | 1 medium | 1 medium | 1 medium |
| Courgette (zucchini) | 1 | 1 | 1 |
| Field mushroom | 1 large | 1 large | 1 large |
| Oil | | | |
| **Tomato stuffing** | | | |
| Canned mushy peas, drained | 75 g | 3 oz | ½ cup |
| Plain yogurt | 1 tbsp | 1 tbsp | 1 tbsp |
| Egg, beaten | 1 | 1 | 1 |
| Salt and freshly milled black pepper | | | |
| **Mushroom stuffing** | | | |
| Cream cheese, softened | 75 g | 3 oz | ⅓ cup |
| Garlic clove, crushed | 1 | 1 | 1 |
| Snipped chives | 1 tbsp | 1 tbsp | 1 tbsp |
| **Aubergine (eggplant) stuffing** | | | |
| Onion, chopped | 1 small | 1 small | 1 small |
| Garlic clove, chopped | 1 | 1 | 1 |
| Walnuts, chopped | 25 g | 1 oz | ¼ cup |
| Oil | 2 tbsp | 2 tbsp | 2 tbsp |
| Coriander leaves, chopped | 1 tbsp | 1 tbsp | 1 tbsp |
| Egg, beaten | 1 | 1 | 1 |
| Salt and freshly milled black pepper | | | |
| **Courgette (zucchini) stuffing** | | | |
| Cooked rice | 50 g | 2 oz | ⅓ cup |

| | | | |
|---|---|---|---|
| *Cooked peas* | *1 tbsp* | *1 tbsp* | *1 tbsp* |
| *Cooked sweetcorn* | *1 tbsp* | *1 tbsp* | *1 tbsp* |
| *(whole kernel corn)* | | | |
| *Raisins* | *1 tbsp* | *1 tbsp* | *1 tbsp* |
| *Ground turmeric* | *1 tsp* | *1 tsp* | *1 tsp* |
| *Salt and freshly milled* | | | |
| *black pepper* | | | |
| *Egg, beaten* | *1* | *1* | *1* |

## method

1.   To fill the tomatoes, first cut a large slice from the end opposite the stem end of each tomato. Remove the seeds with a teaspoon and scoop out the pulp. (Reserve the pulp for the aubergine/eggplant stuffing.)

2.   Blend the mushy peas with the yogurt and egg and season with salt and pepper. Fill the tomatoes with this mixture and place on a baking tray.

3.   For the mushroom stuffing, first remove the mushroom stem and chop. (Reserve the chopped stem for the aubergine/eggplant stuffing.)

4.   Mix the cream cheese, garlic and chives and form into a ball. Put into the centre of the up-turned mushroom cap. Place on the baking tray with the tomatoes.

5.   For the aubergine (eggplant) stuffing, combine the chopped mushroom stem with the onion, garlic and walnuts. Heat the oil in a frying-pan (skillet) and stir-fry this mixture for 5 minutes.

6.   Cut the aubergine in half lengthwise and make diagonal incisions in the flesh. Wash in plenty of water, leave to soak for 2 minutes, then drain and pat dry.

7.   Cook the aubergine halves in boiling water for 5 minutes to soften the flesh, then drain. Scoop the flesh out of the halves, leaving just enough in each to form a firm shell.

8.   Dice the flesh and add it to the cooked mushroom and walnut mixture. Add the tomato pulp and season to taste with salt and pepper and coriander. Leave to cool.

9. Bind the mixture with beaten egg and pack into the two aubergine halves. Place on a second baking tray.

10. Finally, stuff the courgette (zucchini). Cut a slice, lengthwise, leaving two thirds of the courgette and scoop out the pulp to form a cavity.

11. Combine all the stuffing ingredients, seasoning the mixture with salt and pepper and binding with beaten egg. Pack into the courgette and place on the baking tray with the stuffed aubergine.

12. Preheat the oven to 200°C/400°F/Gas Mark 6. Drizzle a little oil over the courgette and aubergines and bake in the oven for 20 minutes.

13. Bake the tomatoes and mushroom for 5-6 minutes or cook under a hot grill (broiler). Serve all the stuffed vegetables together on a platter.

# MEXICAN TACOS

Serve this exciting meal as an informal birthday supper for two.
Corn tacos are now available in packages from supermarkets.
They can be filled with anything you fancy. The filling in this recipe
combines mashed baked beans, avocado and tomato. Another
filling you might like to try is easily made by stirring chopped red
pepper into scrambled egg. You can, of course, double the
ingredients to serve four people.

## Serves 2 — ingredients

| | Metric | Imperial | American |
|---|---|---|---|
| Taco shells | 2 | 2 | 2 |
| Oil | 2 tbsp | 2 tbsp | 2 tbsp |
| Onion, chopped | 1 small | 1 small | 1 small |
| Green chilli (chili pepper), seeded and sliced | 1 | 1 | 1 |
| Baked beans, mashed | 50 g | 2 oz | ¼ cup |
| Avocado, stoned (pitted), peeled and diced | 1 | 1 | 1 |
| Tomato, peeled, seeded and diced | 1 | 1 | 1 |
| Salt and freshly milled black pepper | | | |

## method

1. Place the taco shells in the oven to warm while preparing the filling.

2. Heat the oil in a frying-pan (skillet) and stir-fry the onion and chilli (chili pepper) for 2 minutes. Add the mashed beans and cook 2 minutes more. Stir in the avocado and tomato and season with salt and pepper.

3. Line the taco shells with lettuce leaves and spoon the bean mixture on top. Serve immediately.

# GALETTE DE LENTILLE

## Lentil Patties

These crisp patties are extremely nourishing and delicious eaten with a salad made of strips of vegetable and beansprouts in a vinaigrette dressing.

**Serves 4**

### ingredients

|  | Metric | Imperial | American |
|---|---|---|---|
| Green or split lentils | 225 g | 8 oz | 1 cup |
| Water | 600 ml | 1 pint | 2½ cups |
| Oil |  |  |  |
| Onion, chopped | 1 small | 1 small | 1 small |
| Green chilli (chili pepper), seeded and chopped | 1 | 1 | 1 |
| Pinch of cumin |  |  |  |
| Pinch of ground ginger |  |  |  |
| Pinch of curry powder |  |  |  |
| Salt |  |  |  |
| Egg, beaten | 1 | 1 | 1 |
| Plain yogurt | 2 tbsp | 2 tbsp | 2 tbsp |
| Plain (all-purpose) flour | 2 tbsp | 2 tbsp | 2 tbsp |
| Rolled oats | 100 g | 4 oz | 1¼ cups |

**Salad**

|  | Metric | Imperial | American |
|---|---|---|---|
| Carrot, cut in julienne strips | 1 | 1 | 1 |
| Turnip or mouli (Japanese white radish), cut in julienne strips | 1 | 1 | 1 |
| Beansprouts | 150 g | 5 oz | 2½ cups |

**Dressing**

|  | Metric | Imperial | American |
|---|---|---|---|
| Oil | 2 tbsp | 2 tbsp | 2 tbsp |
| Lemon juice | 2 tbsp | 2 tbsp | 2 tbsp |
| Plain yogurt | 1 tbsp | 1 tbsp | 1 tbsp |
| Salt and freshly milled black pepper |  |  |  |

## method

1.   Place the lentils in a bowl, cover with water and leave to soak for 1 hour.

2.   Drain the lentils well and place in a saucepan with the water. Boil for 20 minutes, then drain and mash to a purée. Leave to cool.

3.   Heat 1 tablespoon oil in a frying-pan (skillet) and stir-fry the onion and chilli for 3 minutes. Sprinkle in the cumin, ginger and curry powder and season with salt.

4.   Blend the lentil purée with the onion and spice mixture, mix well and form into ten large balls. Flatten each to a patty shape.

5.   Beat the egg and yogurt together. Coat the patties in flour, then dip in egg and yogurt. Finally, dip in rolled oats. (If necessary, use a palette knife to retain the shape of the patties.)

6.   Heat oil in a frying-pan and fry the patties for 2-3 minutes until golden brown on both sides. Drain well on absorbent kitchen paper.

7.   To make the vinaigrette dressing, place all the ingredients in a blender or food processor and blend well. Alternatively, place the ingredients in a screw-topped jar and shake well until blended.

8.   Serve the patties with the vegetables and beansprouts tossed in the dressing.

# GOUGERE NICOISE

This festive gougère, made with cheese choux pastry, is filled with a mixture of courgettes (zucchini), tomatoes and French (green) beans.

*Serves 6*

## ingredients

|  | Metric | Imperial | American |
|---|---|---|---|
| **Choux pastry** | | | |
| Polyunsaturated margarine | 50 g | 2 oz | ¼ cup |
| Water | 120 ml | 4 fl oz | ½ cup |
| Pinch of salt | | | |
| Strong plain (all-purpose) flour | 150 g | 5 oz | 1¼ cups |
| Eggs, beaten | 2 | 2 | 2 |
| Gruyère cheese, grated | 100 g | 4 oz | 1 cup |
| **Filling** | | | |
| French (green) beans | 50 g | 2 oz | ½ cup |
| Oil | 50 ml | 2 fl oz | ¼ cup |
| Onion, chopped or sliced | 1 small | 1 small | 1 small |
| Courgettes (zucchini), sliced | 2 | 2 | 2 |
| Tomatoes, peeled, seeded and chopped | 2 | 2 | 2 |
| Peanuts | 50 g | 2 oz | ¼ cup |
| Salt and freshly milled black pepper | | | |
| Chopped fresh parsley | 1 tbsp | 1 tbsp | 1 tbsp |
| Cheese, grated | 3 tbsp | 3 tbsp | 3 tbsp |

## method

1.   First, make the choux pastry. Place the margarine and water in a saucepan, heat gently until the fat has melted, then bring to the boil. Remove the pan from the heat and add the salt and all the flour. Beat thoroughly then return to the heat.

2.   Heat gently, beating all the time, for about 3 minutes until the mixture is smooth and forms a ball in the centre of the pan. Leave to cool for 1-2 minutes.

3.   Beat the eggs into the dough, adding a little at a time, until the dough is soft enough to pipe. When all the egg has been absorbed, stir in the grated cheese.

4.   Preheat the oven to 200°C/400°F/Gas Mark 6. Lightly oil a round 25 cm/10 inch cake tin (pan).

5.   Start piping the choux in the centre of the greased tin and pipe in a spiral until the bottom of the tin is covered.

6.   Next, pipe little buns of choux around the outside edge of the tin as if to make a crown of choux.

7.   Bake in the oven for 30 minutes until risen, golden brown and just firm to the touch.

8.   Meanwhile, make the filling. Cook the French (green) beans in boiling water for 5 minutes, then cut in small pieces.

9.   Heat the oil in a frying-pan (skillet) and stir-fry the onion for 2 minutes. Add the courgettes (zucchini) and tomatoes and cook for 3 minutes until the vegetables are tender but still crunchy. Combine with the peanuts and beans and season with salt and pepper.

10.   When cooked, carefully turn the gougère out of the tin and transfer to a larger 30 cm/12 inch serving plate. Fill with the vegetable mixture, sprinkle with chopped parsley and grated cheese and serve at once.

# CORN AND TOMATO CUPS

These delightful tomato-flavoured baked custards are delicious
served with a mixed salad and jacket potato or French bread.

## Serves 4 — ingredients

|  | Metric | Imperial | American |
|---|---|---|---|
| *Onion, thinly sliced* | 1 | 1 | 1 |
| *Tomatoes, peeled and sliced* | 2 large | 2 large | 2 large |
| *Avocado, stoned (pitted), peeled and sliced* | 1 | 1 | 1 |
| *Sweetcorn (whole kernel corn)* | 50 g | 2 oz | ½ cup |
| *Wholewheat bread slices* | 4 | 4 | 4 |
| *Polyunsaturated margarine, melted* | 50 g | 2 oz | ¼ cup |
| *Eggs, beaten* | 3 | 3 | 3 |
| *Soya milk* | 300 ml | ½ pint | 1¼ cups |
| *Salt and freshly milled black pepper* | | | |
| *Grated (ground) nutmeg* | | | |
| *Gruyère cheese, grated* | 100 g | 4 oz | 1 cup |
| *Toasted sesame (benne) seeds* | | | |

## method

1.  Grease the bottoms of four individual ovenproof dishes.

2.  In the bottom of each dish, arrange onion, tomato and
avocado slices with sweetcorn (whole kernel corn).

3.  Cut the bread slices in small triangles and brush with melted
margarine. Arrange, overlapping, on top of the vegetables in
each dish.

4.  Beat together the eggs and soya milk and season with salt, pepper and nutmeg. Pour over the contents of each dish and leave to soak for 20 minutes. Preheat the oven to 190°C/375°F/Gas Mark 5.

5.  Bake the puddings in the oven for 40 minutes, then remove and sprinkle with grated cheese. Place under a hot grill (broiler) for 3 minutes until golden. Sprinkle with toasted sesame (benne) seeds and serve at once while piping hot.

# CHICKPEA AND SPINACH CASSEROLE

**Serves 4**

## ingredients

| | Metric | Imperial | American |
|---|---|---|---|
| Fresh spinach, stems removed, washed and drained | 450 g | 1 lb | 1 lb |
| Melted butter and oil | 2 tbsp | 2 tbsp | 2 tbsp |
| Garlic clove, chopped | 1 | 1 | 1 |
| Can chickpeas (garbanzos) | 225 g | 8 oz | 8 oz |
| Feta cheese, cut into cubes | 100 g | 4 oz | 1 cup |
| Salt and freshly milled black pepper | | | |
| Sour cream | 100 ml | 4 fl oz | ½ cup |

## method

1.  Shred the spinach leaves. Heat the butter and oil in a saucepan and cook the spinach for 4 minutes.

2.  Add the chickpeas and feta cheese. Season to taste and stir in the sour cream just before serving. This casserole could be served with plain boiled noodles with plenty of grated cheese.

# BEAN CASSOULET TOULOUSE-LAUTREC

The famous French painter was very fond of cassoulet which was a speciality of Toulouse where many members of my family have lived for generations. This recipe omits the meat, of course, but it is just as good. Serve with a cucumber salad with chive and yogurt dressing. Casseroles are ideal festive fare as the cook has more time to concentrate on his or her guests.

*Serves 4*

## ingredients

| | Metric | Imperial | American |
|---|---|---|---|
| Haricot (navy) beans | 225 g | 8 oz | 8 oz |
| Oil | 1 tbsp | 1 tbsp | 1 tbsp |
| Onions, thickly sliced | 2 medium | 2 medium | 2 medium |
| Celery stalks, sliced | 2 | 2 | 2 |
| Red pepper, seeded and chopped | 1 | 1 | 1 |
| Fennel bulb, sliced | 1 | 1 | 1 |
| Garlic cloves, chopped | 3 | 3 | 3 |
| Green chilli (chili pepper), seeded and sliced | 1 small | 1 small | 1 small |
| Red wine | 2 tbsp | 2 tbsp | 2 tbsp |
| Pine nuts | 50 g | 2 oz | ½ cup |
| Sprig of thyme | | | |
| Sprig of marjoram | | | |
| Dijon mustard | 1 tsp | 1 tsp | 1 tsp |
| Vegetable stock (bouillon) cube | 1 | 1 | 1 |
| Tomatoes, peeled, seeded and chopped | 2 large | 2 large | 2 large |
| Wholewheat breadcrumbs | 50 g | 2 oz | ½ cup |
| Grated Cheddar cheese | 75 g | 3 oz | ¾ cup |

## method

1.   Place the beans in a bowl, cover with cold water and leave to soak overnight.

2.   Drain the beans, rinse, drain again and cook in boiling water for 30 minutes. Drain and place in an ovenproof casserole. Preheat the oven to 150°C/300°F/Gas Mark 2.

3.   Heat the oil in a frying-pan (skillet) and stir-fry the onions, celery, pepper, fennel, garlic and chilli for 5 minutes. Add to the beans.

4.   Cover the ingredients of the casserole with water and add the wine, pine nuts, herbs and mustard. Crumble in the stock (bouillon) cube. Cover and bake in the oven for 1½ hours.

5.   Remove the casserole from the oven and increase the temperature to 220°C/425°F/Gas Mark 7.

6.   Spread the chopped tomato on top of the casserole and cover with breadcrumbs. Top with grated cheese. Return, uncovered, to the oven and cook for 12 minutes. Serve straight from the casserole.

# BRUSSELS SPROUTS AND CHESTNUTS COLCANON

This is a special version of the traditional 'Bubble and squeak', using chestnuts instead of potatoes. Delicious served at Christmas time, the addition of yogurt makes the dish even more appealing as it gives it a more creamy flavour. The same dish could be made using cooked cabbage instead of Brussels sprouts.

( Serves 4 ) ── **ingredients**

|  | Metric | Imperial | American |
|---|---|---|---|
| Sunflower oil | 5 tbsp | 5 tbsp | 5 tbsp |
| Chopped onion | 150 g | 5 oz | 1 cup |
| Small fresh or frozen Brussels sprouts, cooked and cooled | 225 g | 8 oz | ½ lb |
| Chestnuts, cooked, peeled and cooled or canned chestnuts, drained | 225 g | 8 oz | ½ lb |
| Peeled and sliced apple | 50 g | 2 oz | ½ cup |
| Peanuts | 50 g | 2 oz | ½ cup |
| Salt and freshly milled black pepper | | | |
| Grated (ground) mace or nutmeg | | | |
| Plain yogurt to serve (optional) | | | |

**method**

1. Heat the oil in a large frying-pan (skillet) and stir-fry the onion for 1 minute until soft but not brown.

2. Add the Brussels sprouts, chestnuts, apple and peanuts. Toss together and fry for 5 minutes until golden.

3.  Season to taste with salt, pepper and mace or nutmeg and serve immediately on individual plates. Drizzle a little yogurt over each portion, if liked.

# SPANISH PAELLA

## Serves 4 — ingredients

| | Metric | Imperial | American |
|---|---|---|---|
| Oil | 3 tbsp | 3 tbsp | 3 tbsp |
| Onion, chopped | 1 | 1 | 1 |
| Long-grain rice | 150 g | 5 oz | 1 cup |
| Turmeric | 1 tsp | 1 tsp | 1 tsp |
| Curry powder | 1 tsp | 1 tsp | 1 tsp |
| Salt to taste | | | |
| Green chilli, sliced | 1 | 1 | 1 |
| Red and green peppers, seeded and diced | 75 g | 3 oz | ¾ cup |
| Garlic cloves, chopped | 2 | 2 | 2 |
| Green olives, stoned | 50 g | 2 oz | ½ cup |
| Water | 500 ml | ¾ pint | 2 cups |
| Vegetable stock (bouillon) cube | 1 | 1 | 1 |
| Tomatoes, skinned, seeded and chopped | 2 | 2 | 2 |
| Pine kernels | 50 g | 2 oz | ½ cup |
| Peas | 50 g | 2 oz | ½ cup |

## method

1.  Preheat the oven to 200°C/400°F/Gas Mark 6.

2.  Place a 1.75 litre/3 pint/7½ cup metal paella pan on the stove and heat the oil. Stir fry the onion for 1 minute, then add the rice, turmeric, curry powder, salt, chilli, peppers, garlic, olives, water and stock cube. Boil for 5 minutes. Add the tomatoes, pine kernels and peas.

3.  Transfer the paella to the oven, cover with a lid and bake for 30-40 minutes.

# FELAFEL JERUSALEM

These little fritters, made from chick-peas (or garbanzos), are the best natural meat replacement you could imagine. The perfect main course for an informal celebration.

## Serves 4 — ingredients

| | Metric | Imperial | American |
|---|---|---|---|
| Canned chick peas, drained | 400 g | 14 oz | 2 cups |
| Red onion, chopped | 1 | 1 | 1 |
| Garlic clove, chopped | 1 | 1 | 1 |
| Green chilli (chili pepper), seeded and chopped | 1 | 1 | 1 |
| Mint leaves, chopped | 3 | 3 | 3 |
| Ground cumin | 1 tsp | 1 tsp | 1 tsp |
| Caraway seeds | 1 tsp | 1 tsp | 1 tsp |
| Plain (all purpose) flour | 75 g | 3 oz | ¾ cup |
| Egg, beaten | 1 | 1 | 1 |
| Oil for shallow frying | | | |
| **To serve** | | | |
| Pita breads | 4 | 4 | 4 |
| Bunch of watercress | | | |
| Avocado | 1 | 1 | 1 |
| Tomatoes | 2 | 2 | 2 |

## method

1.   Combine the chick peas, onion, garlic, chilli, herbs and spices in a blender or food processor. Blend to a paste and transfer to a bowl.

2.   Divide the paste into ten portions and shape into balls. Flatten, coat with flour and dip in beaten egg.

3.   Heat oil in a frying-pan (skillet) and fry the felafel for 4 minutes until golden on both sides. Drain well on absorbent kitchen paper.

4.   To serve, make a cut in the side of each pita bread and open up to form a pocket. Place one or two felafel in each pita and add watercress and slices of avocado and tomato.

# STUFFED PEPPERS

## Serves 4 — ingredients

|  | Metric | Imperial | American |
|---|---|---|---|
| Cold cooked Spanish Paella (see page 51) | 225 g | 8 oz | 8 oz |
| Eggs, beaten | 2 | 2 | 2 |
| Red peppers | 4 | 4 | 4 |

## method

1.   Preheat the oven to 200°C/400°F/Gas Mark 6.

2.   Slice the stems from the peppers and set aside. Make an opening in the pepper tops to remove the seeds with a spoon.

3.   In a bowl, blend the eggs with the cooked Paella. Spoon the mixture into the cavities of the peppers. Stand them in a deep earthenware dish. Part fill the dish with hot water and bake in the oven for 30 minutes. Meanwhile, blanch the pepper top stems and sit them on top of the cooked peppers.

# CHINESE NOODLES AND LYCHEES

A light summer entertaining dish.

**Serves 4**

## ingredients

|  | Metric | Imperial | American |
|---|---|---|---|
| Thin Chinese egg noodles | 225 g | 8 oz | ½ lb |
| **Sauce** | | | |
| Oil | 50 ml | 2 fl oz | ¼ cup |
| Shallots, chopped | 2 small | 2 small | 2 small |
| Red pepper, seeded and diced | 50 g | 2 oz | ½ cup |
| Courgettes (zucchini), sliced | 2 | 2 | 2 |
| Can of lychees, drained | 1 small | 1 small | 1 small |
| Cucumber, diced | 50 g | 2 oz | ½ cup |
| Blanched almonds, toasted | 50 g | 2 oz | ½ cup |
| Plain yogurt | 120 ml | 4 fl oz | ½ cup |
| Salt and freshly milled black pepper | | | |

## method

1.   Cook the noodles in boiling salted water for 5-8 minutes, then drain well.

2.   For the sauce, heat the oil in a frying-pan (skillet) and stir-fry the shallots and red pepper for 3 minutes. Add the courgettes (zucchini), lychees, cucumber and almonds and cook for 2 minutes more.

3.   Stir in the yogurt, heat until warmed through and season to taste with salt and pepper.

4.   Divide the noodles between four heated serving plates and pour over the sauce. Serve at once.

# 3

# Salads

---

## JAMAICAN CITRUS SALAD

This refreshing salad is packed with plenty of vitamin C.

**Serves 4**

### ingredients

| | Metric | Imperial | American |
|---|---|---|---|
| Lettuce leaves | 4 | 4 | 4 |
| Seedless oranges, peeled, pith removed and segmented | 2 | 2 | 2 |
| Grapefruit, peeled, pith and pips (seeds) removed and segmented | 1 | 1 | 1 |
| Red kidney beans or pigeon peas, cooked | 75 g | 3 oz | ⅓ cup |
| Beansprouts | 75 g | 3 oz | 1½ cups |
| **Dressing** | | | |
| Plain yogurt | 75 ml | 2½ fl oz | 5 tbsp |
| Juice of 1 lemon | | | |
| Salt and freshly milled black pepper | | | |

### method

1.  To make the dressing, beat the yogurt and lemon juice togther and season with salt and pepper.

2.  Arrange the lettuce leaves on two serving plates and arrange the fruit segments on top. Sprinkle the beans and beansprouts all over. Serve the dressing separately.

# RICE PINEAPPLE SALAD

This colourful rice salad makes a popular addition to a party buffet. The flavour of ginger and pineapple is enhanced by the combination of all the ingredients. You can easily double the ingredients for a larger gathering.

## Serves 4 — ingredients

|  | Metric | Imperial | American |
|---|---|---|---|
| Cooked rice, drained | 75 g | 3 oz | ⅔ cup |
| Pineapple slices, preferably fresh, cubed | 2 | 2 | 2 |
| Mushrooms, wiped and sliced | 4 | 4 | 4 |
| Celery stalk, sliced | 1 | 1 | 1 |
| Cucumber, cubed | 75 g | 3 oz | ¾ cup |
| Green chilli (chili pepper), seeded and sliced | 1 | 1 | 1 |
| **Dressing** | | | |
| Peanuts | 25 g | 1 oz | 1 tbsp |
| Lemon juice | 2 tbsp | 2 tbsp | 2 tbsp |
| Oil | 1 tbsp | 1 tbsp | 1 tbsp |
| Salt and freshly milled black pepper | | | |
| Pineapple juice | 2 tbsp | 2 tbsp | 2 tbsp |
| Fresh root ginger, peeled and grated | 1 tsp | 1 tsp | 1 tsp |
| **Garnish** | | | |
| Watercress | | | |
| Toasted peanuts | | | |

## method

1.  First make the dressing. Place all the ingredients in a blender or food processor and blend well.

2.  Combine the salad ingredients in a bowl and add a little dressing. Toss and serve on individual plates garnished with watercress and toasted peanuts.

# HOT MUSHROOM SALAD

*Serves 4*

## ingredients

|  | Metric | Imperial | American |
|---|---|---|---|
| *Field mushrooms* | *225 g* | *8 oz* | *2 cups* |
| *Olive oil* | *4 tbsp* | *4 tbsp* | *4 tbsp* |
| *Small sprig thyme* | *1* | *1* | *1* |
| *Salt and freshly milled black pepper* | | | |
| *Garlic cloves, chopped* | *2* | *2* | *2* |
| *Small fried bread croûtons* | | | |
| *Wine vinegar* | *2 tbsp* | *2 tbsp* | *2 tbsp* |
| *A selection of salad leaves to serve.* | | | |

## method

1.  Clean and trim the mushrooms. Wash and drain, then cut in thin slices or quarter.

2.  Heat the oil in a wok and stir-fry the mushrooms and thyme for 1 minute only. Season to taste and add the garlic and fried croûtons. Toss for 30 seconds, then remove the thyme.

3.  Divide the mushrooms onto 4 plates over the salad leaves. Drizzle a little vinegar over the salad mixture just before serving.

# SALADE AUX COQUILETTES

This exquisite and attractive salad combines pasta shells with mouli, radishes and tangerines on a bed of lettuce or Chinese leaves. Pasta is a good way to introduce cereal protein into your diet.

## Serves 4 — ingredients

|  | Metric | Imperial | American |
|---|---|---|---|
| Pasta shells | 225 g | 8 oz | ½ lb |
| Mouli (Japanese white radish), peeled and cut in 6 mm/¼ inch cubes | 1 | 1 | 1 |
| Bunch of radishes, sliced | 1 | 1 | 1 |
| Cucumber, cut in 6 mm/¼ inch cubes | ¼ | ¼ | ¼ |
| Salt and freshly milled black pepper |  |  |  |
| Lettuce leaves or Chinese leaves | 8 | 8 | 8 |
| Black olives, stoned (pitted ripe olives) | 4 | 4 | 4 |
| Tangerines, peeled and segmented | 2 | 2 | 2 |
| **Dressing** |  |  |  |
| Garlic clove | 1 | 1 | 1 |
| Tomato, peeled, seeded and cubed | 1 | 1 | 1 |
| Walnut oil | 2 tbsp | 2 tbsp | 2 tbsp |
| Wine vinegar | 1 tbsp | 1 tbsp | 1 tbsp |

## method

1.  First make the dressing. Place all the ingredients in a blender or food processor and blend well.

2.   Cook the pasta shells in boiling water for 8 minutes. Drain, refresh in cold water until cold, then drain again.

3.   Combine the pasta, mouli, radishes and cucumber in a salad bowl. Add dressing, season with salt and pepper and toss well.

4.   Line individual serving plates with lettuce or Chinese leaves and pile salad on top. Garnish with olives and tangerine segments. Serve any remaining dressing separately.

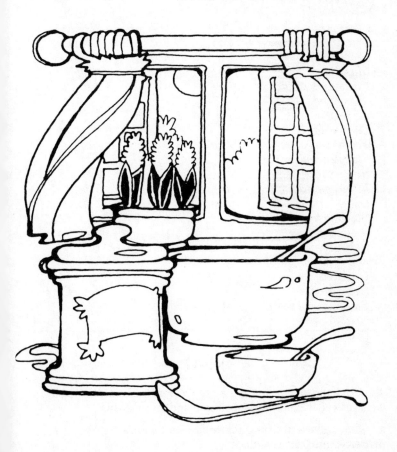

# VERMICELLI SALAD NANKIN STYLE

A tempting pasta salad tossed in ginger, pineapple and soya sauce dressing.

## Serves 4 — ingredients

|  | Metric | Imperial | American |
|---|---|---|---|
| *Vermicelli, tagliatelle or linguini* | *225 g* | *8 oz* | *½ lb* |
| *Mushrooms, sliced* | *100 g* | *4 oz* | *1 cup* |
| *Cooked chestnuts (canned will do)* | *100 g* | *4 oz* | *¼ lb* |
| **Dressing** |  |  |  |
| *Fresh root ginger, peeled and grated* | *1 tsp* | *1 tsp* | *1 tsp* |
| *Soya sauce* | *1 tbsp* | *1 tbsp* | *1 tbsp* |
| *Pineapple juice* | *5 tbsp* | *5 tbsp* | *5 tbsp* |
| *Oil* | *2 tbsp* | *2 tbsp* | *2 tbsp* |
| *Salt and freshly milled black pepper* |  |  |  |
| *Garlic clove* | *1* | *1* | *1* |
| **Garnish** |  |  |  |
| *Beansprouts* | *100 g* | *4 oz* | *2 cups* |
| *Sprigs of watercress* |  |  |  |

## method

1. Cook the pasta in boiling salted water for 5 minutes. Drain well, refresh in cold water until cold and drain again.

2. Place all the dressing ingredients in a blender or food processor and blend well.

3.  Place the mushrooms and chestnuts in a bowl, pour over the dressing and leave to marinate for 10 minutes. Add the pasta and mix well.

4.  Arrange the salad on individual serving plates and garnish with beansprouts and watercress.

# NEW POTATO SALAD

## Serves 4 — ingredients

|                                    | Metric  | Imperial | American |
| ---------------------------------- | ------- | -------- | -------- |
| New potatoes                       | 450 g   | 1 lb     | 1 lb     |
| Watercress leaves                  | 150 g   | 5 oz     | 5 oz     |
| Spring onions (scallions), chopped | 4       | 4        | 4        |
| **Dressing**                       |         |          |          |
| Egg yolks                          | 2       | 2        | 2        |
| Salt and freshly milled black pepper |       |          |          |
| Made Dijon mustard                 | ½ tsp   | ½ tsp    | ½ tsp    |
| Oil                                | 3 tbsp  | 3 tbsp   | 3 tbsp   |
| Sour cream                         | 3 tbsp  | 3 tbsp   | 3 tbsp   |
| Juice of 1 lemon                   |         |          |          |
| Mixed salad leaves to serve        |         |          |          |

## method

1.  Boil the new potatoes for 20 minutes. Peel while still hot. Cut in slices and place in a large bowl.

2.  Wash, drain and pat dry the watercress leaves and add to the potatoes with the onions.

3.  In a bowl, place the egg yolks with salt and pepper and made mustard. Whisk while adding the oil in a small thread until the mixture thickens. Then blend in the cream and lemon juice.

4.  While still warm, toss the salad gently with this dressing. Divide between 4 plates, adorned with mixed salad leaves.

# SALADE LILLOISE

This salad, which is made of chicory (endive), was a speciality of my late brother, Pierre, who used to own a Café Routier in Lille. If liked, sprinkle the finished salad with croûtons just before serving, and you could try dandelion leaves instead of spinach or chard. Serve as a side salad or as part of a buffet spread.

## Serves 4 — ingredients

|  | Metric | Imperial | American |
|---|---|---|---|
| Chicory (endive) heads | 4 | 4 | 4 |
| Spinach or chard leaves, shredded | 225 g | 8 oz | 8 oz |
| Sliced button mushrooms | 75 g | 3 oz | ¾ cup |
| Walnuts | 150 g | 5 oz | 1¼ cups |
| **Dressing** | | | |
| Mayonnaise | 75 ml | 2½ fl oz | 5 tbsp |
| Grated rind and juice of 1 lemon | | | |
| Sour cream | 2 tbsp | 2 tbsp | 2 tbsp |
| Apple purée (applesauce) | 2 tbsp | 2 tbsp | 2 tbsp |

## method

1. First make the dressing. Place all the ingredients in a blender or food processor and blend well.

2. Separate two of the chicory (endive) heads into leaves and slice the remaining two. Mix the sliced chicory with the spinach or chard, mushrooms and walnuts. Toss in one third of the dressing.

3. Serve the salad on individual plates garnished with chicory leaves. Serve the remaining dressing separately.

# 4

# *D*esserts

---

## APRICOT COULIS

This coulis can be made with other stone fruits, such as peaches, nectarines or plums. Use to accompany puddings, rice desserts, pancakes or fritters.

| Serves 4 — **ingredients** | Metric | Imperial | American |
|---|---|---|---|
| Fresh apricots | 450 g | 1 lb | 1 lb |
| Sweet white wine or sweet sherry | 150 ml | ¼ pint | ⅔ cup |
| Granulated sugar | 50 g | 2 oz | ¼ cup |
| Kirsch or Cointreau | 2 tbsp | 2 tbsp | 2 tbsp |

### method

1. Wash and drain the apricots. Remove the stones.

2. Boil the apricots, wine and sugar until soft, about 4 minutes. Liquidise the mixture to a purée or pass through a nylong sieve. Lastly, add the Kirsch or Cointreau.

# APPLE AND BLACKCURRANT KISSEL

This festive dessert is made in all Scandinavian and Russian countries, served with yogurt or sour cream. If fresh blackcurrants are not available, used canned, or use blackcurrant syrup and omit the sugar from this recipe.

## Serves 4 — ingredients

|  | Metric | Imperial | American |
|---|---|---|---|
| Cooking (tart) apples, cored, peeled and sliced | 3 | 3 | 3 |
| Blackcurrants | 150 g | 5 oz | 1¼ cups |
| Sugar | 100 g | 4 oz | ½ cup |
| Potato flour | 2 tsp | 2 tsp | 2 tsp |
| Water | 5 tbsp | 5 tbsp | 5 tbsp |
| Pinch of ground cinnamon | | | |
| Red wine (preferably port wine) | 150 ml | ¼ pint | ⅔ cup |
| Plain yogurt or sour cream to serve | | | |

## method

1.   Place the apples and blackcurrants in a saucepan with the sugar, cover and cook until the apples are soft. Pour the mixture into a blender or food processor and blend to a smooth purée. Return to the saucepan.

2.   Blend the potato flour with the water, stir into the purée and re-boil, stirring, until thickened. Flavour with a little cinnamon and wine.

3.   Serve cold in individual glasses or bowls with yogurt or sour cream (slightly whipped, if liked).

# PEARS IN WHITE WINE WITH PASSION FRUIT PUREE

This unusual pear dessert will introduce you to the passion fruit. Never mind the seeds — they are good fibre! Simply double the ingredients for four people.

## Serves 2 — ingredients

|  | Metric | Imperial | American |
|---|---|---|---|
| *Very ripe dessert pears, cored, peeled and quartered* | 2 large | 2 large | 2 large |
| *Passion fruit* | 4 | 4 | 4 |
| *Sweet white wine, such as Graves or Sauternes* | 300 ml | ½ pint | 1¼ cups |
| *Honey* | 1 tbsp | 1 tbsp | 1 tbsp |
| *Cornflour (cornstarch)* | ¼ tsp | ¼ tsp | ¼ tsp |
| *Water* | 4 tbsp | 4 tbsp | 4 tbsp |
| *Juice of ½ lemon or lime, if necessary* | | | |
| *Langues de chats or other biscuits to serve (see page 68)* | | | |

## method

1.   Place the pears in two serving glasses or dishes. Cut the passion fruit in half and scoop out the pulp into a small bowl.

2.   Bring the wine and honey to the boil. Blend the cornflour (cornstarch) with the water and stir into the syrup when boiling. Simmer for 5 minutes to clear the starch, then add the passion fruit pulp. Boil for 1 minute more. Add the juice of half a lemon or lime if not acid enough.

3.   Pour the sauce over the pears and leave to cool. Serve with langues de chats or other biscuits.

# RASPBERRY YOGURT SORBET WITH APPLE AND KIWI FRUIT SALAD

In summer, use fresh raspberries instead of canned. Add a little water when puréeing them.

## Serves 4 — ingredients

|  | Metric | Imperial | American |
|---|---|---|---|
| Canned raspberries | 225 g | 8 oz | ½ lb |
| Sugar | 100 g | 4 oz | ½ cup |
| Egg whites | 2 | 2 | 2 |
| Plain (very firm) yogurt | 150 ml | 5 fl oz | ⅔ cup |
| **Salad** | | | |
| Kiwi fruit, (Chinese gooseberries), sliced | 2 | 2 | 2 |
| Green eating apples, cored, peeled and sliced | 2 | 2 | 2 |
| Kirsch or bottled lime juice to taste | | | |

## method

1.   Place the raspberries in a blender or food processor with their juice and blend to a purée. Pour into a saucepan, add the sugar and boil for 2 minutes. Leave to cool.

2.   Beat the egg whites until stiff and fold into the raspberry purée, then fold in the yogurt. Pour into a freezer container and freeze for 3 hours.

3.   Remove from the freezer and beat the sorbet (sherbet) to break down ice crystals, then re-freeze for at least another 3 hours until firm.

4.   To serve, scoop sorbet onto plates and garnish with a salad of fruit. Sprinkle a little Kirsch or lime juice over the fruit.

# BRANDY SNAP HORNS AND BASKETS

Pretty, yet versatile, these elegant brandy snap shapes can be filled with cream and fruit — just before serving.

**Serves 4** — **ingredients**

|  | Metric | Imperial | American |
|---|---|---|---|
| Butter | 100 g | 4 oz | ½ cup |
| Brown sugar | 100 g | 4 oz | ½ cup |
| Golden syrup (light corn syrup) | 100 g | 4 oz | ⅓ cup |
| Ground ginger | 1 tsp | 1 tsp | 1 tsp |
| Plain (all-purpose) flour | 100 g | 4 oz | 1 cup |
| Lemon juice | 1 tsp | 1 tsp | 1 tsp |
| Orange juice | 1 tsp | 1 tsp | 1 tsp |

**method**

1. Grease one or two baking sheets. Preheat the oven to 200°C/ 400°F/Gas Mark 6.

2. Place the butter, sugar, syrup and ginger in a saucepan and heat gently until melted. Add the flour and mix well. Stir in the lemon and orange juice.

3. Drop small spoonfuls of the mixture onto baking sheets, allowing plenty of room for expansion between each one. Bake in the oven for a few minutes until bubbly and golden.

4. While still hot, remove the rounds from the baking sheets and roll around greased cream horn tins (pans). Leave in place until set, then twist gently to remove and leave to cool. Alternatively, place the hot rounds in greased fluted bun tins (fluted muffin pans) and leave to set.

# LITTLE BASKETS OF FRUIT

This gourmet dessert, with baskets made of langues de chats biscuit mixture, can be varied by using different fruits to make the sauce and fill the baskets. You could even make two sauces and pour half of each on each plate for a very special effect. Avoid using fruits with too much moisture to fill the baskets.

## Serves 4 — ingredients

|  | Metric | Imperial | American |
|---|---|---|---|
| **Langues de chats biscuit mixture** |  |  |  |
| Icing (confectioner's) sugar, sifted | 100 g | 4 oz | ¾ cup |
| Flour, sifted | 100 g | 4 oz | 1 cup |
| Ground almonds | 25 g | 1 oz | ¼ cup |
| Egg whites | 3 | 3 | 3 |
| Pinch of salt |  |  |  |
| **Mango sauce** |  |  |  |
| Mango, halved and stoned (pitted) | 1 | 1 | 1 |
| Juice of 1 lime |  |  |  |
| Sugar | 25 g | 1 oz | 2 tbsp |
| White wine | 75 ml | 2½ fl oz | 5 tbsp |
| Cornflour (cornstarch) | ½ tsp | ½ tsp | ½ tsp |
| Water | 5 tbsp | 5 tbsp | 5 tbsp |
| **Fresh fruits** |  |  |  |
| Assorted fresh fruits, such as sliced banana, cubed pineapple, strawberries or raspberries, halved grapes | 450 g | 1 lb | 1 lb |
| **Decoration** |  |  |  |
| Icing (confectioner's) sugar |  |  |  |
| Fresh mint leaves |  |  |  |

## method

1. Preheat the oven to 190°C/375°F/Gas Mark 5. Grease two baking sheets and place four 18 cm/7 inch flan rings on them.

2. For the biscuit mixture, place all the ingredients in a bowl and beat together to form a creamy batter.

3. Spoon the batter into the four flan rings and spread evenly. Bake in the oven for 8-9 minutes until golden.

4. Remove the cooked biscuits from the rings and baking sheet immediately and, while still hot, place each on top of an inverted small heatproof mixing bowl. Let fall or mould (mold) them into a cup shape. Leave to cool until firm.

5. For the sauce, scoop the pulp out of the mango halves and place in a saucepan with the lime juice, sugar and wine. Bring to the boil, then purée in a blender or food processor. Return to the pan.

6. Blend the cornflour (cornstarch) with the water and stir into the mango purée. Cook for 4 minutes, stirring, until thickened. Pour a pool of sauce onto four serving plates.

7. Handling the biscuit baskets very carefully, position one on top of the sauce on each plate. Fill the baskets with mixed fruit and dust with icing (confectioner's) sugar. Decorate each with a mint leaf.

# GATEAU DE NOEL AUX MARRONS GLACES FLAMBE AU RHUM

In my view, this chocolate gâteau will go down better than Christmas pudding and, displayed on a platter surrounded by flowers, will make an ideal showpiece for your main Christmas meal. It is not complicated to make and can be made in advance and stored in the freezer until the day of joy. Of course, this impressive gâteau can be served at any festive occasion.

## Serves 12

### ingredients

|  | Metric | Imperial | American |
|---|---|---|---|
| Eggs | 6 large | 6 large | 6 large |
| Caster (superfine) sugar | 150 g | 5 oz | ⅔ cup |
| Self-raising flour | 100 g | 4 oz | 1 cup |
| Cocoa powder (unsweetened cocoa) | 40 g | 1½ oz | 3 tbsp |
| Baking powder | 1 tsp | 1 tsp | 1 tsp |
| Flaked (slivered) almonds, toasted and ground | 50 g | 2 oz | ½ cup |

**Jam filling**

| | | | |
|---|---|---|---|
| Thick apricot or peach jam | 225 g | 8 oz | ½ lb |
| Spirit (liquor) of your choice (optional), e.g. Kirsch, rum, brandy, gin or whisky | 2 tbsp | 2 tbsp | 2 tbsp |

**Butter cream filling**

| | | | |
|---|---|---|---|
| Unsalted (sweet) butter | 150 g | 5 oz | ⅔ cup |
| Sour cream or plain yogurt | 1 tbsp | 1 tbsp | 1 tbsp |
| Icing (confectioner's) sugar, sifted | 100 g | 4 oz | ¾ cup |

| | | | |
|---|---|---|---|
| Chopped hazelnuts, toasted and ground | 100 g | 4 oz | 1 cup |
| Cocoa powder (unsweetened cocoa) | ½ tbsp | ½ tbsp | ½ tbsp |
| Grated plain (semi-sweet) chocolate | 1 tbsp | 1 tbsp | 1 tbsp |
| Rum or Grand Marnier to taste | | | |

**Ganache cream covering**

| | | | |
|---|---|---|---|
| Single (light) cream | 300 ml | ½ pint | 1¼ cups |
| Grated plain (semi-sweet) chocolate | 225 g | 8 oz | ½ lb |
| Rum or Grand Marnier | 2 tbsp | 2 tbsp | 2 tbsp |

**Decoration**

| | | | |
|---|---|---|---|
| Marrons glacés | 12 | 12 | 12 |
| Glacé (candied) cherries, halved | 6 | 6 | 6 |
| Sugar-coated pralines | 12 | 12 | 12 |
| Gold or silver cake ribbon | | | |
| Xmas cake decoration, e.g. Father Xmas figure or 'Merry Xmas' | | | |

## method

1. Preheat the oven to 200°C/400°F/Gas Mark 6. Grease and line with greaseproof (waxed) paper a round 20 cm/8 inch cake tin (pan) that is 9 cm/3½ inches deep.

2. Using a hand-held electric whisk or an electric mixer, cream the eggs and sugar together at high speed for 8 minutes until light and fluffy and the beaters leave a trail in the mixture when lifted.

3. Sift together the flour, cocoa, baking powder and ground almonds. Fold into the mixture in three portions, mixing gently with a metal spoon to retain the lightness of the mixture.

4.   Pour the mixture into the prepared tin, level with a spatula and bake in the centre of the oven for 50 minutes.

5.   Leave the cooked cake to cool for 15 minutes before inverting onto a wire rack to cool completely. When cold, carefully peel off the lining paper and split the cold cake horizontally in three layers. Place one layer on a 28 cm/11 inch cake board and the other two on wire racks for easy handling.

6.   For the jam filling, blend the jam with 2 tablespoons water and bring to the boil. Add the spirit (liquor) of your choice, if using. Remove from the heat and leave until just warm.

7.   To make the butter cream, beat together the butter, sour cream or yogurt and icing (confectioner's) sugar until fluffy. Beat in the hazelnuts and cocoa. Finally beat in the chocolate. The mixture should be light like whipped cream. Flavour with a little rum or Grand Marnier.

8.   For the ganache cream, bring the cream to the boil and add the grated chocolate. Simmer until the chocolate has melted and is well blended. Cool and beat until it is of a fluffy piping consistency. Add the rum or Grand Marnier.

9.   Spread the first cake layer (on the board) with half of the warm jam mixture and spread the remainder over another sponge layer. Leave to cool completely.

10.   When the jam is cold, cover both layers with butter cream and place the second on the top of the first, covered side up. Place the third sponge layer on top and cover the whole cake, top and sides with ganache cream. Smooth over with a palette knife.

11.   Place the remaining butter cream in a piping (pastry) bag fitted with a small star nozzle and pipe a scroll around the top edge. Decorate the gâteau with marrons glacés, cherries and different coloured pralines. Freeze the gâteau to harden the butter cream and ganache.

12.   Before serving, remove the gâteau from the freezer and tie a gold or silver ribbon around it. Place the Xmas decoration in the centre and serve on a silver platter. To cut, dip a large cake knife in hot water and cut into 12 or 16 slices, dipping the knife in hot water between each cut.

# APPLE AND CRANBERRY CLAFOUTIS

*Baked Apple and Cranberry Pudding*

This is a traditional dessert from the French region of Limosin. It makes a satisfying conclusion to a wintertime dinner party.

## Serves 6 — ingredients

|  | Metric | Imperial | American |
|---|---|---|---|
| *Wholewheat flour* | *150 g* | *5 oz* | *1¼ cups* |
| *Good pinch of salt* | | | |
| *Brown sugar* | *100 g* | *4 oz* | *⅔ cup* |
| *Eggs, beaten* | *4 large* | *4 large* | *4 large* |
| *Milk or single (light) cream, or half milk and half cream* | *350 ml* | *12 fl oz* | *1½ cups* |
| *Cranberries, washed* | *450 g* | *1 lb* | *1 lb* |
| *Apples, cored, peeled and sliced* | *225 g* | *8 oz* | *½ lb* |
| *Icing (confectioner's) sugar, sifted* | *50 g* | *2 oz* | *½ cup* |

## method

1.   Grease a large 16 cm/6½ inch flan tin which is 4 cm/¾ inch deep, smothering bottom and sides with margarine. Preheat the oven to 200°C/400°F/Gas Mark 6.

2.   Place the flour, salt and sugar in a bowl and mix together. Beat the eggs and milk or cream together and add gradually to the flour, beating well to form a smooth batter.

3.   Arrange the fruits in the bottom of the flan tin and pour over the batter. Bake in the centre of the oven for 45 minutes.

4.   Invert onto a dish and cut in wedges. Dust with icing (confectioner's) sugar just before serving.

# CREPES SUZETTE AUX PECHES FLAMBEES WITH CHERRY BRANDY

*Crêpes Suzette with Peaches Flamed with Cherry Brandy*

Cherry Jubilee has been done to death since the late King George V was honoured with this dish. Much water has passed under the bridge since then and other fancies have been created to amaze guests who like to see a firework display of desserts ignited with brandy. Here is my version which combines thin crêpes in a lovely orange syrup with peaches and red Morello (sour) cherries. The crêpes can be made well in advance and stored on a plate in the refrigerator until you are ready for your firework display! Use other exotic fruits, if preferred, such as pineapples, bananas, kiwi fruits or mangos. The perfect dessert for that special birthday dinner party.

**Serves 4**

## ingredients

| | Metric | Imperial | American |
|---|---|---|---|
| Eggs, beaten | 2 | 2 | 2 |
| Milk | 150 ml | ¼ pint | ⅔ cup |
| Water | 150 ml | ¼ pint | ⅔ cup |
| Plain (all-purpose) flour | 100 g | 4 oz | 1 cup |
| Oil | 1 tsp | 1 tsp | 1 tsp |
| Pinch of salt | | | |
| Oil for cooking | | | |
| Butter | 50 g | 2 oz | ¼ cup |
| Sugar | 50 g | 2 oz | ¼ cup |
| Sugar cubes | 2 | 2 | 2 |
| Pinch of ground cinnamon | | | |
| Grated rind of ½ and juice of 1 orange | | | |
| Yellow peaches, halved and stoned (pitted) | 4 | 4 | 4 |

| | | | |
|---|---|---|---|
| Can of Morello (sour) cherries, drained and stoned (pitted) | 1 small | 1 small | 1 small |
| Brandy | 50 ml | 2 fl oz | ¼ cup |
| Cherry Brandy liqueur | 50 ml | 2 fl oz | ¼ cup |

## method

1.   To make the crêpe batter, beat together the eggs, milk and water, blend in the flour and beat until smooth. Add the oil and salt and leave for 30 minutes.

2.   Heat a little oil in a non-stick 12 cm/5 inch omelette pan and pour in enough batter to cover the bottom of the pan. Cook until golden on the underside, then toss or turn and cook the other side. Slide onto a sheet of greaseproof (waxed) paper and leave to cool. Repeat until you have made eight crêpes. When cold, store in the refrigerator until required.

3.   When ready to serve, first make a syrup by melting the butter and sugar together in a large sauté pan. Boil for 4 minutes, adding cinnamon and orange rind and juice, to form a butterscotch syrup.

4.   Dip each crêpe in the butterscotch to warm, then fold in quarters and arrange on a flameproof serving platter or metal dish. Pour over the remaining syrup and surround the crêpes with peaches and cherries.

5.   Pour the brandy over the crêpes and heat until boiling. Ignite and then extinguish the flames with Cherry Brandy. Serve each guest with two crêpes, one peach and a spoonful of syrup and cherries.

# FRUIT PIZZA

The surprise in this dessert pizza is delicious crème pâtissière.

## Serves 4 — ingredients

|  | Metric | Imperial | American |
|---|---|---|---|
| Packet (package) pizza dough mix | 1 | 1 | 1 |
| Plain yogurt to serve | | | |

**Crème pâtissière (Confectioner's custard)**

|  | Metric | Imperial | American |
|---|---|---|---|
| Egg yolks | 2 | 2 | 2 |
| Caster (superfine) sugar | 50 g | 2 oz | ¼ cup |
| Plain (all-purpose) flour | 2 tbsp | 2 tbsp | 2 tbsp |
| Cornflour (cornstarch) | 2 tbsp | 2 tbsp | 2 tbsp |
| Milk | 300 ml | ½ pint | 1¼ cups |
| Few drops of vanilla essence | | | |

**Decoration**
Seedless grapes
Bananas
Orange segments
Apple slices
Apricot jam to glaze

## method

1. First make the crème pâtissière. Cream eggs and sugar together until thick and pale. Sift flour and cornflour (cornstarch) together into the bowl and beat in, adding a little cold milk to make a smooth paste.

2. Heat the remaining milk in a saucepan until almost boiling and pour onto the egg mixture, stirring continuously. Reheat, stirring, until the mixture boils. Add vanilla to taste and cook for a further 2-3 minutes. Cover and leave to cool.

3.  Make up the pizza dough as directed on the packet (package) and roll out to a 20 cm/8 inch round. Place on a greased baking sheet. Preheat the oven to 200°C/400°F/Gas Mark 6.

4.  Spread the dough round thinly with crème pâtissière and bake in the oven for 10 minutes. Leave to cool.

5.  When cold, decorate with fruit. Place the apricot jam in a saucepan with a little water, heat gently, stirring, until the jam melts, then simmer for 1 minute. Strain and brush over the fruits while still warm.

6.  Place the pizza under the grill (broiler) until the fruit just starts to colour. Serve hot with yogurt.

# FRUIT CHOUX DELIGHT

A gourmet dessert of choux buns filled with Crème St. Honoré and a
variety of fresh fruits.

**Serves 4**

## ingredients

| | Metric | Imperial | American |
|---|---|---|---|
| *Choux pastry (see page 44)* | | | |
| *Apricot jam to glaze* | | | |
| *Curaçao to serve* | | | |
| | | | |
| **Crème St. Honoré** | | | |
| *Caster (superfine) sugar* | 225 g | 8 oz | 1 cup |
| *Egg whites, stiffly beaten* | 2 | 2 | 2 |
| *Egg yolks* | 2 | 2 | 2 |
| *Milk* | 150 ml | ¼ pint | ⅔ cup |
| *Few drops of vanilla essence* | | | |

**English fruit filling**
*Apples*
*Blackcurrants*
*Raspberries*
*Strawberries*

**Tropical fruit filling**
*Mango*
*Lime*
*Banana*

**Exotic fruit filling**
*Kiwi fruit (Chinese gooseberries)*
*Lychees*
*Ginger*

---
## method
---

1.   Preheat the oven to 220°C/425°F/Gas Mark 7. Grease a baking sheet.

2.   Spoon the choux pastry into a piping (pastry) bag fitted with a star nozzle and pipe round rosettes onto the baking sheet. Bake in the oven for 25-30 minutes until crisp.

3.   When cooked, remove the choux buns from the oven and cut horizontally in two. Place the top halves upside-down on the bottom halves. Leave to cool.

4.   To make the Crème St. Honoré, boil the sugar in a little water for about 5 minutes until at the 'soft boil stage' (113-118°C/235-245°F), or until a small drop of syrup can be rolled into soft ball when dropped in cold water.

5.   Whisk (beat) egg whites until stiff then pour in the hot syrup.

6.   Place egg yolks and milk in a saucepan and heat gently, whisking (beating) until starting to thicken. Add the meringue and syrup mixture and flavour with vanilla. Spoon into a piping (pastry) bag.

7.   Pipe Crème St. Honoré onto the bottom halves of the choux buns and top with fruit mixture of your choice. Brush the tops with boiled, strained apricot jam and serve straight away with a glass of Curaçao.

**Variation**
Pipe the choux in banana shapes. Cut in half lengthwise after baking. Fill bottoms with Crème St. Honoré and top with raspberries. turn top half upside-down and place on top of raspberries. Fill with Crème St. Honoré and place one whole peeled banana, cut in half lengthwise, on top. Brush with apricot glaze, spin chocolate across the top and sprinkle with split almonds.

# UNE MELONADE AUX FRUITS

Adding exotic fruits to this refreshing dessert will provide colour and charisma to any celebration meal, try papayas (pawpaws), kiwi fruit and lychees. Lace the whole mixture with your favourite liqueurs, mixed — Grand Marnier, Cointreau or Kirsch. Add a few seeds of pomegranate and you have a splendid dessert.

## Serves 4 — ingredients

|  | Metric | Imperial | American |
|---|---|---|---|
| Melons, halved, seeded and peeled | 2 small | 2 small | 2 small |
| Papaya (pawpaw), peeled, seeded and sliced | 1 | 1 | 1 |
| Kiwi fruit (Chinese gooseberries), peeled and sliced | 4 | 4 | 4 |
| Fresh lychees or canned, drained | 225 g | 8 oz | ½ lb |
| Strawberries, hulled and halved | 225 g | 8 oz | ½ lb |
| Bananas, peeled and sliced | 2 | 2 | 2 |
| Tangerines, peeled and segmented | 4 | 4 | 4 |
| Caster (superfine) sugar or honey to taste (optional) |  |  |  |
| Mixed nuts, peeled, e.g. pine nuts, walnuts, flaked (slivered) almonds, pistachios |  |  |  |
| Large bunch of fresh mint or lemon balm leaves |  |  |  |
| Grand Marnier, Cointreau or Kirsch, mixed | 75 ml | 2½ fl oz | 5 tbsp |

| Pomegranate | 1 | 1 | 1 |
| Sour or whipped cream to serve | | | |

## method

1. Place the melon halves on four serving plates and arrange the other fruits decoratively on and around the melon. Add honey or sugar, if necessary. Sprinkle with nuts and finish with sprigs of mint or lemon balm leaves.

2. Just before serving, sprinkle with the liqueur mixture. Cut the pomegranate in wedges and place one on each plate, or sprinkle with the seeds only. Serve with sour or whipped cream.

# ROYAL SABAYON AU COGNAC

Keep this rich Italian dessert for that special celebration. It can be served warm or cold in large 200 ml/⅓ pint/⅞ cup glasses with petits fours or langues de chats biscuits (see page 68). Some petits fours can easily be made with marzipan. Stuff dates and soaked prunes with small balls of marzipan and dip in granulated sugar. Other delicious petits fours can be made by dipping fruits in toffee. You could also buy petits fours such as Turkish Delight and macaroons.

## Serves 4 — ingredients

| | Metric | Imperial | American |
|---|---|---|---|
| Egg yolks | 4 | 4 | 4 |
| Eggs, beaten | 2 | 2 | 2 |
| Caster (superfine) sugar | 50 g | 2 oz | ¼ cup |
| Cognac | 50 ml | 2 fl oz | ¼ cup |
| Cointreau | 25 ml | 1 fl oz | 2 tbsp |
| Sweet white wine | 75 ml | 2½ fl oz | 5 tbsp |
| Orange juice | 75 ml | 2½ fl oz | 5 tbsp |
| Grated rind and juice of 1 lime or 1 lemon | | | |

**Decoration**
Mint leaves
Strawberries
Kiwi fruit
  (Chinese
  gooseberries)

## method

1.   Place the egg yolks, beaten eggs and sugar in a heatproof bowl and beat for 4 minutes with a balloon whisk.

2.   Place the bowl over a saucepan of boiling water and whisk for 5 minutes until the mixture thickens like custard. Gradually whisk in Cognac and Cointreau.

3.    Pour the wine and orange juice into a saucepan with the rind and juice of a lime or lemon and warm without boiling. Gradually pour into the custard, whisking all the time.

4.    Leave the mixture to thicken in the bowl over the heat to prevent curdling. Pour into large balloon glasses to serve.

5.    If you prefer a frothy Sabayon, whisk two egg whites with a pinch of salt until thick, then fold into the wine custard before pouring into glasses.

6.    Decorate the glasses with mint leaves, slices of strawberry and kiwi fruit (Chinese gooseberry) and serve immediately with langues de chats biscuits or petits fours.

# 5
▼
# *D*rinks

## NOISETTINE WITH WHISKY

A festive nut, honey and whisky drink diluted with orange and ginger ale.

### Serves 4 — ingredients

| | Metric | Imperial | American |
|---|---|---|---|
| Blanched almonds | 25 g | 1 oz | ¼ cup |
| Walnuts | 25 g | 1 oz | ¼ cup |
| Peanuts | 25 g | 1 oz | ¼ cup |
| Honey | 2 tbsp | 2 tbsp | 2 tbsp |
| Whisky | 75 ml | 2½ fl oz | 5 tbsp |
| Ice cubes | 3 | 3 | 3 |
| Juice of 2 oranges | | | |
| Ginger ale | 300 ml | ½ pint | 1¼ cups |
| Orange slices | 4 | 4 | 4 |
| Kiwi fruit, (Chinese gooseberry), sliced | 1 | 1 | 1 |

### method

1. Place the nuts, honey, whisky, ice cubes and orange juice in a blender or food processor and blend well.

2. Pour into four medium glasses and top up with ginger ale. Serve decorated with slices of orange and kiwi fruit (Chinese gooseberry).

# MORELLO BRANDY FIZZ

<table>
<tr><td>Serves 4</td><td colspan="4">ingredients</td></tr>
<tr><td></td><td>Metric</td><td>Imperial</td><td>American</td></tr>
<tr><td>Morello (sour) cherries, canned</td><td>400 g</td><td>14 oz</td><td>3½ cups</td></tr>
<tr><td>Carbonated mineral water</td><td>300 ml</td><td>½ pint</td><td>1¼ cups</td></tr>
<tr><td>Brandy</td><td>150 ml</td><td>¼ pint</td><td>⅔ cup</td></tr>
<tr><td>Ice cubes</td><td>3</td><td>3</td><td>3</td></tr>
<tr><td>Orange slices</td><td>4</td><td>4</td><td>4</td></tr>
</table>

## method

1. Drain the can of cherries, reserving cherries and juice.

2. Place 300 ml/½ pint/1¼ cups cherry juice in a large jug (pitcher) and add the remaining ingredients, including the reserved cherries. Stir well and serve.

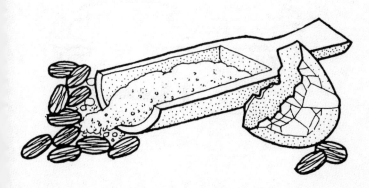

# TEQUILA A LA SANCHO

| Serves 4 | ingredients | | |
|---|---|---|---|
| | Metric | Imperial | American |
| Ice cubes | 8 | 8 | 8 |
| Grenadine | 4 tbsp | 4 tbsp | 4 tbsp |
| Crème de banane | 4 tbsp | 4 tbsp | 4 tbsp |
| Tequila | 120 ml | 4 fl oz | ½ cup |
| Double (heavy) cream | 4 tbsp | 4 tbsp | 4 tbsp |

## method

1. Place two ice cubes in each of four glasses and add 1 tablespoon Grenadine followed by 1 tablespoon crème de banane and 2 tablespoons tequila.

2. Top each glass with 1 tablespoon cream and serve.

**Variation**
For a less pungent drink, dilute with ginger ale and purée in a blender or food processor with two ripe bananas.

# PEACH AND PINEAPPLE PUNCH

**Serves 14**

## ingredients

|  | Metric | Imperial | American |
|---|---|---|---|
| Lemons | 2 | 2 | 2 |
| Limes | 2 | 2 | 2 |
| Oranges | 2 | 2 | 2 |
| Water | 1.75 litres | 3 pints | 7½ cups |
| Heather honey | 300 ml | ½ pint | 1¼ cups |
| Pineapple slices | 3 | 3 | 3 |
| Peaches | 4 large | 4 large | 4 large |
| Bunch of black (purple) grapes, seeded | 1 small | 1 small | 1 small |
| Strong tea | 300 ml | ½ pint | 1¼ cups |
| Cloves | 6 | 6 | 6 |
| Cinnamon stick | 1 | 1 | 1 |
| Brandy or whisky | 300 ml | ½ pint | 1¼ cups |

## method

1.    Squeeze the juice from the lemons, limes and oranges and pare the rind from one lemon, one lime and one orange. Reserve the juice and place the rind in a saucepan with the water. Bring to the boil and stir in the honey until dissolved. Simmer for 5 minutes.

2.    Remove from the heat and stir in the lemon, lime and orange juice. Add all the remaining ingredients and stir well.

3.    Chill the punch for at least 3 hours and transfer to a large punch bowl to serve.

# SCANDINAVIAN JULGLOGG

This is a traditional Christmas punch which is usually served with Danish pastries. It would make a warming addition to any wintertime special occasion.

## Serves 8

### ingredients

|  | Metric | Imperial | American |
|---|---|---|---|
| Red wine | 1.5 litres | 2½ pints | 6¼ cups |
| Seedless grapes or raisins | 100 g | 4 oz | ¾ cup |
| Honey | 100 g | 4 oz | ⅓ cup |
| Cardamom seeds | 12 g | ½ oz | 3 tbsp |
| Cloves | 4 | 4 | 4 |
| Cinnamon stick | 1 | 1 | 1 |
| Grated rind of 1 lemon |  |  |  |
| Grated rind of 1 lime |  |  |  |
| Aquavit | 1 litre | 1¾ pints | 4 cups |

### method

1.   Place the red wine, grapes or raisins, honey, cardamom seeds, cloves and cinnamon in a large saucepan and bring to the boil.

2.   Remove from the heat and add the lemon and lime rinds and the Aquavit.

3.   Just before serving, reheat gently and ignite. Serve in punch cups. If preferred, the spices may be removed with a slotted spoon.

# VIN CHAUD AUX FRAMBOISES

## *Raspberry Mulled Wine*

This delightful hot mulled wine has been served in my family for centuries.

**Serves 6**

### ingredients

|  | Metric | Imperial | American |
|---|---|---|---|
| Raspberries, fresh, frozen or drained canned | 150 g | 5 oz | 1 cup |
| Brandy | 75 ml | 2½ fl oz | 5 tbsp |
| Bottle red Bordeaux wine | 1 | 1 | 1 |
| Cinnamon stick | 1 | 1 | 1 |
| Honey | 75 g | 3 oz | ¼ cup |

### method

1.   Place the raspberries in a bowl, add the brandy and leave to soak. (If using canned raspberries, add the juice also.)

2.   Place the wine and cinnamon in a saucepan and bring to the boil. Boil for 2 minutes, then add the honey and stir until dissolved.

3.   Purée the raspberries and brandy in a blender or food processor and add to the wine mixture.

4.   Remove the cinnamon and serve the hot mulled wine in punch cups.

# MUSCADET CASSIS

This is a delightful and refreshing wine cup which is not too alcoholic. It is very popular in France as an aperitif or as a drink to serve with a special meal.

**Serves 6**

## ingredients

|  | Metric | Imperial | American |
|---|---|---|---|
| *Bottle Muscadet white wine* | 1 | 1 | 1 |
| *Ice cubes* | 3 | 3 | 3 |
| *Lime slices* | 4 | 4 | 4 |
| *Blackcurrant syrup (Cassis)* | 75 ml | 2½ fl oz | 5 tbsp |

## method

1. Place all the ingredients in a 1.2 litre/2 pint/5 cup jug (pitcher) and mix well.

2. Pour into glasses to serve.

# PAPINO WITH PAPAYA

## Serves 4

### ingredients

|  | Metric | Imperial | American |
|---|---|---|---|
| Milk | 600 ml | 1 pint | 2½ cups |
| Lemon sorbet (sherbet) | 50 ml | 2 fl oz | ¼ cup |
| Papaya (pawpaw), peeled, seeded and sliced | 1 | 1 | 1 |
| Juice of 1 lime |  |  |  |
| Ice cubes | 2 | 2 | 2 |
| Mint or borage leaves to decorate |  |  |  |

### method

1. Place all ingredients in a blender or food processor and blend well.

2. Pour into four tall glasses, decorate with mint or borage leaves and serve at once. Alternatively, reserve slices of papaya (pawpaw) and lime to decorate.

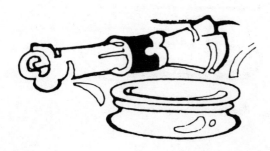

# PINEAPPLE AND CRANBERRY MILK SHAKE

**Serves 4**

## ingredients

|  | Metric | Imperial | American |
|---|---|---|---|
| Soya milk | 600 ml | 1 pint | 2½ cups |
| Pineapple slices | 2 | 2 | 2 |
| Honey | 1 tbsp | 1 tbsp | 1 tbsp |
| Cranberries | 50 g | 2 oz | ½ cup |
| Ice cubes | 3 | 3 | 3 |
| Apple and orange slices to decorate | | | |

## method

1. Place all the ingredients in a blender or food processor and blend for 2 minutes.

2. Pour into four tall glasses, decorate with apple and orange slices and serve at once.

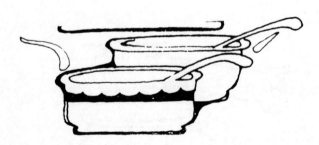

# GRENADINE ORANGEADE

Pomegranates have a rich red juice and flavour and a syrup called Grenadine is made from them.

*Serves 4*

## ingredients

|  | Metric | Imperial | American |
|---|---|---|---|
| Orange juice | 300 ml | ½ pint | 1¼ cups |
| Ginger ale | 300 ml | ½ pint | 1¼ cups |
| Grenadine syrup | 50 ml | 2 fl oz | ¼ cup |
| Pomegranate to decorate |  |  |  |

## method

1. Place the orange juice in a cocktail shaker or large jug (pitcher) and top up with ginger ale.

2. Add the Grenadine syrup and mix well.

3. Cut the pomegranate into thin wedges and add to the drink before serving.

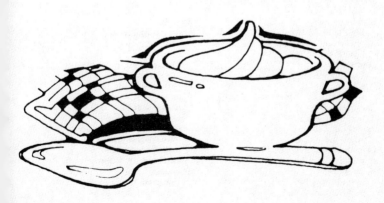

# INDEX

# INDEX